The Park Cities

A portion of a 1900 map of Dallas drawn by Sam Street shows the area that became the Park Cities. Near the middle of the map the name J. Cole is next to Exall Lake, on the mid-left is Exall's Lomo Alto Farm, and near the upper right is the location of the Caruth Farm. The dotted lines indicate wagon roads.

The PARK Cities

A Walker's Guide
& Brief History

DIANE GALLOWAY

KATHY MATTHEWS

Illustrations by Patricia McMillan
Maps by Barbara Jezek

Southern Methodist University Press

FIRST EDITION, 1988

Requests for permission to reproduce material from
this work should be sent to:
Permissions
Southern Methodist University Press
Box 415
Dallas, Texas 75275

Library of Congress Cataloging-in-Publication Data
Galloway, Diane.
The park cities.

Includes index.
1. Walking—Texas—Highland Park (Dallas)—Guide-
books.   2. Walking—Texas—University Park (Dallas)—
Guide-books.   3. Highland Park (Dallas, Tex.)—
History.   4. University Park (Dallas, Tex.)—History.
5. Highland Park (Dallas, Tex.)—Description.
6. University Park (Dallas, Tex.)—Description.
I. Matthews, Kathy, 1950–   . II. Title.
GV199.42.T492H544   1988   917.64'2811   88-42634
ISBN 0-87074-276-0 (pbk.)

Designed by Whitehead & Whitehead

Contents

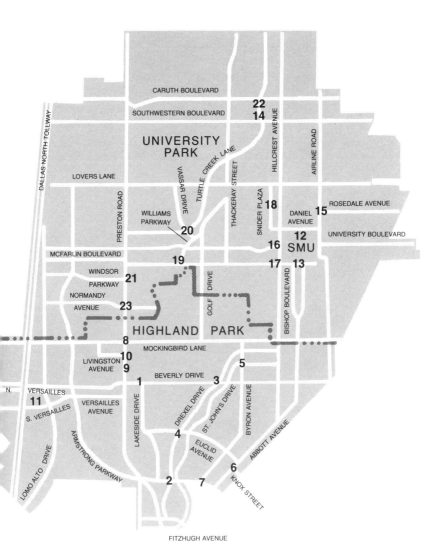

Foreword and Forewarning

Persons attempting to find a motive in this narrative will be prosecuted; persons attempting to find a moral in it will be banished; persons attempting to find a plot in it will be shot.
—Mark Twain, Introduction to *Huckleberry Finn*

THE AUTHORS, like Mark Twain, want to forewarn you that we hope the reader does not expect to find a plot in this book; and we didn't deliberately tack on a moral, although the reader might occasionally find one in the lessons of history. We do, however, have a motive, and we hope you'll find it an honorable one—our desire to share with the reader our fascination with the history of this place we live in called the Park Cities.

In order to avoid any possible misunderstanding, the authors want to make clear from the outset that the history of the Park Cities you find here is just a beginning. The more we researched, the more we realized what a growing, amorphous creature history really is. The answer to one question simply leads to another question and the chain continues. History is a fascinating, frustrating, intriguing subject which tends to change as the identity of the storyteller changes.

In the face of obvious conflicts in data and remembrances, we've done our best to find the "truth," which is often elusive. What you read on the following pages is the most accurate information we could find after countless hours of research, plus a few mysteries we've left unsolved. We genuinely hope that those who have more material or recollections about some of the events and the people herein will come forward to share it with us, for we hope to update and correct this edition as the years pass.

The twenty-three walks in this book can be read in any order, but at least a quick reading of the Exall Lake Walk might serve as an introduction to the early history of the Park Cities. If a place we describe has been bulldozed, we offer our apologies to the reader and save for private conversations our feelings about said bulldozer.

For a more complete description of the various architectural styles seen in the Park Cities, the authors strongly recommend *A Field Guide to American Houses* by Virginia and Lee McAlester.

Highland Park and University Park are now and always have been separately incorporated cities, separate from each other and from the city of Dallas. The map of the Park Cities indicates the boundaries that divide them from each other and from Dallas.

While the city of University Park stands on 3.7 square miles with a population of 22,254, the town of Highland Park is much smaller with 2.2 square miles populated by 8,950 citizens (1980 census). Each has its separate government, but shares the Highland Park Independent School District.

When the book refers to "Highland Park West," it is a historical description of that general area of Highland Park west of Preston Road which opened for development in 1924. Throughout the book this continues to be the meaning, and the only meaning, of that term.

To thank every person who has been helpful in making this book possible would take up most of the rest of the book, because the support and enthusiasm we have encountered have been tremendous. We're deeply indebted to all these supporters, and wish we could mention them all.

It has been our pleasure to have the opportunity to become acquainted with many of the fine citizens of the Park Cities who, with their families, have played such an important role in its development. Special thanks go to Bill Crook for his generosity with his time in reading the manuscript, and his enthusiasm and humor in sharing his recollections, and to La Vern Lankford for her original study for the Cub Scouts which inspired this book. Harriett Clarke, Martha Jean Beaty, Pierce Allman, Lynn Vogt, Olivia Blessing, Betty Littlejohn, Lindalyn Adams, and countless members of the Park Cities Historical Society provided valuable information and help. Jack Kirven generously loaned material about University Park and shared his memories. Thanks also to Dorothy Volk and to Leonard Volk, Hugh Prather, Jr., Lucy Ball Owsley, Mrs. Charles Dilbeck, Mr. and Mrs. Frank Austin, Mrs. Henry Exall, Bill and Max Daniel, Harrison Cave, Jr., Daniel Otstott, Dr. Claude Albritton, Jr., Jeremy Adams, Marty Prince Nichols, Peggy Mims, Tony Briggle, Virginia Perkins Worthington, Bud Oglesby, Taylor Armstrong, Prudence Mackintosh, Muriel McCarthy, Ed Wood, Arles Bynum, Bill and Candy Schoppe, Mrs. John McPolan, Gerald Herman of the YMCA, Mr. and Mrs. George Lee, Jr., and Jim Allums and Stan Knight for their legal advice.

Others who have been a great help are Bonnie Case and her efficient staff at the Highland Park Library, Ronnie Brown and Margie Shelton of the Town of Highland Park, Jaunda Hensley and Jim Murphy at the University Park City Hall, Virginia McAlester for her architectural expertise, Sandra Tyler of the McCulloch Middle School Library, Dr. Ken Thomas and Jana Nazari of Armstrong School, Dr. Louis Powers and Simonne Sumrall of Hyer School, Jean Hudon of the Dallas Public Library, Nina Nixon and Peter Farnham of Old City Park, Charles Embordino of the Dallas Country Club, David Dillon, Marilyn Salmons of the First RepublicBank Park Cities, Carolyn Clarke of Texas Commerce Bank, Ralph Porter Company, and Bradley Photographers.

Particularly helpful at SMU have been Hal Williams, Darwin Payne, Dawn Letson of the DeGolyer Library, Lee Milazzo and Virginia Bols of the SMU

Archives, Elyse Feller of the SMU *Mustang* Magazine, Claire Roberts of the SMU Alumni Office, and Keith Gregory and Suzanne Comer of SMU Press. Freddie Goff of SMU Press did a masterful job of editing our manuscript. Special thanks to Marjorie Waters of the *Park Cities News* for her interest in the book.

And finally, we want to thank our families and friends for their patience and support during the busy times. We hope that the duties we sometimes neglected will soon be forgotten, but that what we were busy about will be remembered.

The Park Cities

"Ten Degrees Cooler"

FROM THE BEGINNING it had an aura about it—
this place we call the Park Cities. In its earliest days it
was a haven for troops hiding from the Indians, when
tired and thirsty soldiers came upon a natural spring
near the "creek with all the turtles." The land that is
now Highland Park was once rolling fields and riding
trails, and later a country outing spot with a steamboat chugging along the banks of Exall Lake. Ten degrees cooler, it claimed, than that rough and dusty,
sometimes wild and woolly city of Dallas, its sylvan
setting provided the inspiration for a community of
parks and well-kept homes. Its idealism and hopes
for the future are symbolized in a single pecan tree in
the very heart of the town.

And its neighbor, University Park, is bonded in the
traditions of education and culture of a once-sleepy
university town. When Robert S. Hyer first stood on
a grassy mound in the middle of a prairie, on the spot
upon which Southern Methodist University's Dallas
Hall would one day be built, perhaps he envisioned
the possibilities to come. Not only SMU, but the city
that sprang up around it, became part of the mys-
tique of what is fondly and otherwise known as "The
Bubble."

With the Katy Railroad providing a window to the
rest of the world; with Highland Park Village, its
unique shopping center, bringing in the latest de-
signer influences on fads and fashions; with the prestigious Dallas Country Club to cater to those interested in society, or at least in golf; and with strict
zoning regulations and housing codes to ensure the

quality of its physical development, the Park Cities grew into a sophisticated and rather unusual community, as the city of Dallas sprawled around it. And Dallas, which once spurned each community's efforts to become a part of it, lived to regret the early decisions not to annex the cities within a city.

But it is the characters in the story of the Park Cities that make it fascinating—those men and women whose dreams and visions shaped it, whose sweat and strength built it; those families who staked their fortunes on the belief that this was a land worth cultivating, a community worth developing, with children worth educating by the best possible means.

Each of the founding families brought divergent ideas to contribute to their community. Yet there seems to be a thread running throughout—a certain pride, a striving to make it better yet for the next generation, to leave a legacy of above the ordinary in life. Sometimes that legacy has been lost. Sometimes dreams have been shattered along the way. But all in all, the wealth and beauty of the land in the Park Cities, the gracious homes and abundant parks and gardens, bespeak the continuation of a dream—of creating an oasis in the midst of a once rather untamed gateway to the West.

The Park Cities has its skeletons in the closet like any other community, but truth is, it's those very skeletons, as well as the respectable folk, who've made this more than just a walking tour. It is history come alive with stories of journeys west and soldiers marching to war, of outrageous wealth and pioneer hardship, of colorful eccentrics and clever business tycoons, of dreamers and doers and dandies. It is their story that we wish to tell in our book as we bring to life the colorful past of the Park Cities while pointing out the sights of the present day.

Walk with us, then, along the trails and through the parks and past the historic—and the ordinary—homes. In these twenty-three walks, we offer the reader a peek at the past, a first-hand look at the present, and a glimpse of things to come in an area that appeals not only to its own residents but to anyone who is interested in history, in colorful characters, in architecture, and in a unique slice of American life.

The Park Cities

Exall Lake Walk

*Among the jolly outings of the week was a hayride and
moonlight picnic at Exall's Lake. . . . a colored band went
along, furnishing music for the ride, a charming sail on the
lake and an "al fresco" dance on the new platform just
erected. The dancing, which was interspersed with choice
refreshments, wound up a dashing cake walk, which made
the fun run at a merry pace until the midnight hour.*
—*Beau Monde* magazine, July 1900

IN THE 1890s Exall Lake became a favorite picnic
and boating spot for Dallasites, but it was so far out in
the country that an outing there was an all-day affair.
Oak Lawn Avenue, the route to Exall Lake, was a
rough gravel road with no houses. The lake boasted
a boathouse where for a quarter you could rent a
boat and fish all day. In those days there were good
catches of bass and perch, and a steamboat even ran
up and down the lake. Later a streetcar line brought
city folks to a stop on Knox Street near the railroad
tracks, but if as many as ten people wanted to go
on to Exall Lake, the conductor would take them
to a spot where they could hike across the fields to
the lake.

Col. Henry Exall, early settler, soldier, and businessman, planned to develop this land, with an
emphasis on parks and parkways, and sell lots for
homes. The development, backed by a group of fi-
nanciers from Philadelphia called the Philadelphia
Place Land Association, was to be called Philadelphia
Place. But the Panic of 1893 caused Exall to lose his
backers, forcing him to sell off a large part of the land.
Several years later, businessman John Armstrong
bought the land, developed it, and called it Highland

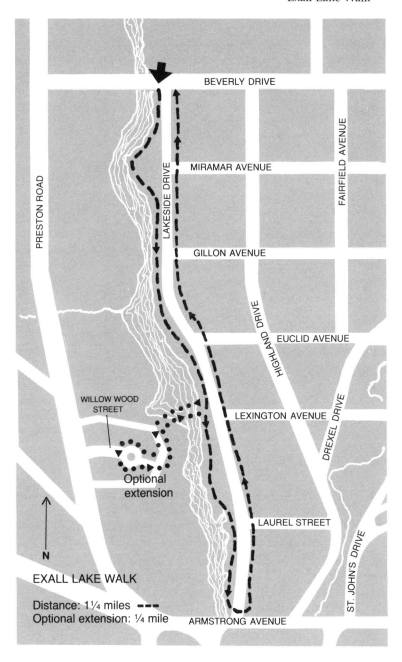

EXALL LAKE WALK

Distance: 1¼ miles ▬▬▬
Optional extension: ¼ mile

Park. Had the recession not hit, Highland Park might be called Philadelphia Place instead, and the homes would be Victorian and Colonial rather than the European period styles seen today.

The men of SMU's Omega Phi fraternity (now called Kappa Sigma) entertain their lady friends on a jolly outing to Exall Lake.

A trip to Lakeside Drive was one of the few off-campus excursions permitted in 1917. *Courtesy of the SMU Archives*

Exall Lake Walk

IT IS FITTING that our first walk in the Park Cities begins by Turtle Creek, because the first Anglo-Americans in the area are believed to have stopped here. When Lt. A. B. Benthuyson's troop of eighteen Texas Rangers was attacked by Indians in 1837, survivors sought refuge east of the Trinity River, finally resting alongside a stream. The men called the stream "the creek with all the turtles." Today Turtle Creek is one of the most beautiful areas of Dallas, especially along Lakeside Drive in the spring when the azaleas and dogwoods bloom in profusion, turning its banks into a blaze of color.

Begin your walk at the intersection of Beverly and Lakeside. Stand facing south at the bridge (dated 1911) and try to imagine nothing here but the creek flowing through a small canyon. That's the way Col. Henry Exall found it when he arrived in 1886. A year later he purchased an option on 1,326 acres of land originally owned by the Cole family along the creek south of Mockingbird Lane. Soon he was growing wheat where Highland Park Village stands today. On a business trip to Philadelphia with his friend Col. J. T. Trezevant, Exall heard about a proposed parkland community there, which gave him the idea for a similar development near Turtle Creek. This scenic area was so near Dallas that he believed he could develop the land and sell houses to the city's well-to-do. In 1889 the Philadelphia Place Land Association bought his option for $500,000, and Exall, acting as their agent, put in gravel roads and built a dam on the creek in 1890 to create Exall Lake. The *Dallas Morning News* called the sale "the biggest single deal in suburban real estate ever made in Texas."

At that time everybody who was anybody in Dallas lived near Ross Avenue. William Caruth, who had developed that first residential subdivision, lived at Ross and St. Paul, the W. H. Flippen home was at Ross and Akard, and the family of Capt. William H. Prather lived nearby. Exall himself lived at Ross and Harwood, near the John Armstrong family at Ross and Pearl. Exall hoped to lure wealthy families such as these to his new parklike development along Turtle Creek, about four miles north of the Dallas courthouse.

By the 1890s, however, a business slump had begun in the United States that would change the history of Highland Park. The story goes that after Dallas lost five banks and cotton dropped four cents a pound in the Panic of 1893, Exall lost everything but his horse. He had to sell off a large part of the Philadelphia Place land. Thanks to the horse, however, he later recouped his fortune. For the next thirteen years he operated the Lomo Alto Horse Farm and bred horses on the land that he retained north of Mockingbird. His stallion Electrite was sought after throughout the Southwest as a stud and in 1897 was named "Champion Sire of the World."

Col. Exall also promoted the horse races that were a main attraction at the State Fair of Texas, of which he was president in 1889. (John Armstrong, who would soon found Highland Park, had been its president in 1888 and held the office again in 1890.) To train his horses for the races, Exall built a racetrack where Preston Center is today. But in 1904 the Texas legislature banned horse racing, which had been the major source of profit at the Fair, and the Fair Association sold the park property to the City of Dallas.

Col. Henry Exall's interest in horses and racing is reflected in this 1912 caricature. *Courtesy of Lynn Vogt*

The Armstrong family is one of the most important families in the history of the Park Cities. They not only were responsible for creating Highland Park but also played a part in founding the Highland Park Independent School District and Southern Methodist University. When John Armstrong moved to Dallas in 1884 from Kentucky, he invested in a wholesale grocery business with Tom Marsalis. Armstrong and Marsalis also bought two thousand acres south of the Trinity and began selling lots in Oak Cliff. After the two men split up, Armstrong retained the grocery business and developed it into a successful meat-packing company. A versatile entrepreneur, he also became president of the City National Bank, a forerunner of InterFirst Bank, presently called First Republic. By 1906 Armstrong had sold his meat-packing plant to Armour, and with that money he bought the land that Exall had hoped to develop.

Meanwhile, Armstrong's two daughters had married their neighbors' sons on Ross, Edgar Flippen and Hugh Prather, and Armstrong quickly put them to work. Armstrong wanted to carry out the idea of a parklike, exclusive planned community, so he and Prather went to California to hire landscape architect Wilbur David Cook, who was designing the glamorous new Los Angeles community of Beverly Hills. John Armstrong's sons-in-law were destined to implement his plan, for in April of 1908 Armstrong died.

Begin walking south on Lakeside from the bridge, and follow the sidewalk down to the lake. In the 1890s this entire area was under water, and the lake was called Lake Neoma on an old map. A longtime resident remembers swimming here with his friends as a boy, without a bathing suit, of course, because he didn't own one, and there were hardly any homes in the area anyway. One evening the swimmers were making a little too much noise and one of the few neighbors called the Highland Park police. An officer rode over on a bicycle to ask them to leave. By the time the officer arrived, the boys had donned their clothes and, though they were still dripping wet because they had no towels, somehow managed to convince him of their innocence. One of these boys would become the governor of Texas. He has bought a home near his favorite swimming hole and owns the swans you may see occasionally on the lake today.

As the land around the lake began to sell, part of the lake itself was filled in to provide more lots, and Lakeside Drive was born. The 6.6-acre estate across from you is the Ed Cox estate, formerly owned by socialite Rose Lloyd.

Wilbur David Cook was not impressed with the land west of Preston, which was relatively treeless prairie farmed by the Cole family, so the development of Old Highland Park began east of Preston in 1907 in a section bounded by Abbott, Armstrong, Drexel, and Gillon. It was natural that this be the First Addition developed, for civilization seemed to stop where the trolley tracks stopped on Knox Street. The first three homes were all built on Lexington because it was so near the trolley tracks. In 1910 Flippen and Prather opened a Second Addition for development here along Lakeside from Turtle Creek to Hackberry Creek, with Dallas Country Club soon to be the new drawing card. In 1915 a Third Addition opened east of Dallas Country Club to Hackberry Creek, and in 1917 a Fourth Addition east of Hackberry Creek. Development of Highland Park east of Preston was nearly completed by the time Highland Park West opened in 1924.

Take a little time to enjoy the natural beauty of the area. As you follow the sidewalk along the lake, you'll notice the ducks. Around October the migrating birds start arriving, including the beautiful wood duck, pintails, occasional blue herons, and the magnificent Canada geese. Don't be tempted to leave your pet Easter duck here; wild ducks are better suited for survival.

At the foot of Gillon Avenue is an area called Simons Point, with a plaque in memory of the man who willed his estate to Highland Park in 1975. (See the Pecan Tree Walk for more about Pollard Simons.) Step down to the lake to get a better view of the back of this 7.7-acre estate at 4800 Preston, which now belongs to Governor Bill Clements. Looking past the tennis court, you'll see a gray mansion built in 1910 by Edgar Flippen as a replica of Mount Vernon to promote this elite, ultra-fashionable subdivision as well as to serve as Flippen's home. It was designed and constructed by C. D. Hill and has been remodeled several times.

Continue walking south past the next street, Euclid. After you pass two giant cottonwood trees on your left, you'll be approaching the footbridge overlooking the

The home at 4800 Preston Road was built in 1910 by Edgar Flippen as a replica of Mount Vernon to promote Highland Park. *Courtesy of the Dallas Public Library*

dam. A marker to the north of the bridge names Exall Lake, 1890. In 1947 when the Town of Highland Park was doing a little work on Exall Dam to prevent overflows, the workmen found a nearly forgotten cornerstone and placed it to the southeast side of the bridge for those interested to see. Unfortunately it has been defaced, but the date is 1890. Notice the hand-carved letters on this stone, which marks the earliest beginnings of Highland Park.

For an optional extension to your walk, cross the recently repaired bridge with its new decking. On the other side you'll see the old pump house at the location of a water well drilled in 1923 for Highland Park's water supply. The pump house currently is used for storage and contains a small Park and Recreation Department office. **Continue past the pump house and turn left to reach a secluded circle of homes that actually is just off Preston Road, on Willow Wood. Then retrace your steps and cross back over the bridge.**

Continue your walk on the east side of the lake. Just south of the 1890 stone marker by the bridge, where Lexington meets Lakeside, is the site of the Old Gill Well. You will find three pipes sticking out of a semicircular stone wall. Each one had a spigot, and people would come from miles around to fill their bottles with the medicinal sulfur water. Ladies in their long dresses would gather here to drink the water and chat, then hurry home to let the water do its magic. It was supposed to cure irregularity and arthritis—and, some even said, impotency, lying, and hooky. Some years ago Red Bolding, manager of research and development for the Dallas Water Department, found out what that water really contained: magnesium sulfate (Epsom salts), calcium sulfate (gypsum), sodium chloride (salt), and hydrogen sulfide (sulfur or the rotten-egg smell). Consider the plight of the young hooky-player caught skipping school. It's a bet that he was cured before the water ever touched his lips!

Continue walking south along the creek to the area at the foot of Laurel Street. You may already have observed several spots near the creek where water still seeps from underground. In May of 1851 William Terry Edmondson was hiding from Indians when he discovered a spring—and a lucky find it was, for the weather had been very dry and the settlers were in need of water. Negro slaves used to believe that water from this spring could make wishes come true. It has been preserved as a wishing well, with wood decking and a bench beside it, and it's still a refreshing spot for a break. Edmondson installed a grist mill at the town of Cedar Springs. He didn't know it when he discovered the spring, but his grandson, Hugh Prather, would be one of the developers of Highland Park. Edmondson's daughter Anne Elizabeth married Capt. William Harrison Prather, a Confederate veteran.

Across the creek from the wishing well is the backyard of real estate developer Trammell Crow at 4500 Preston, formerly the H. L. Edwards mansion. H. L. Edwards was one of the original founders of the Dallas Golf and Country Club. His daughter, Betty, remembers that her father kept a gas pump in the garage because they were so far from Dallas. Across Preston Road from their home was a big farm that was treeless except for one pecan tree. She had a pony cart in which she would wander around these fields picking up stray goats to return to their owners. Once during World War I, the Royal Flying Corps was training in Fort Worth and landed in these open fields. Betty invited them all over for tea. When they discovered that the Edwardses had Scotch, they came back often, using the pecan tree to locate where to land.

4412 Lakeside

The backyard at 4500 Preston is where the first resident of Highland Park, John Cole, built a log cabin in the 1840s. Cole died in 1851, the same year that Edmondson found the spring. (For more about Cole, see the Pecan Tree Walk.)

Continue to the left of the huge, white-trunked syca-more tree and climb some winding steps to follow the path to Armstrong. You can get only glimpses of the property at 4400 Preston, across the creek at the corner of Preston and Armstrong, where John Cole had his orchard. On the bridge is marked the name Neoma, the original name of Exall Lake.

Cross to the east side of Lakeside for a better view of the historic homes on this street. Continue north on Lakeside all the way back to Beverly. The Park Cities Historical Society is considering designating the entire Lakeside area as a historic district. When the Lakeside section of Highland Park opened in 1910, the most popular style for grand homes was Italian Renaissance. You will see this style in abundance on Lakeside, although its popularity declined rapidly after World War I. Italian Renaissance houses are almost always made of stone, stucco, or yellow brick, with wide overhanging eaves supported by decorative brackets. These houses are usually symmetrical, with arches above doors and first-story windows, and the second-story windows are generally smaller.

The Colonial Revival–style home at 4408 Lakeside has simple ornamentation seen only in its shutters and doors. At 4412 is the gray residence formerly owned by real estate developer Henry S. Miller, in the popular Italian Renais-

4500 Lakeside

sance style with arched windows across the porch. Notice the typical wide overhang and small upper windows, as well as the decorative medallions along the belt course (the continuous band running horizontally across the facade). The house at 4416 Lakeside, another Italian Renaissance, was built in 1913. At 4500 is the home of banker and financier Bum Bright, designed by architect Anton Korn in the Spanish Mission style, with an arcaded porch and wide overhang. It was built before World War I, probably in 1918; after the war the Spanish Eclectic style came into vogue. Bunker Hunt, well-known oil man and philanthropist, resides at 4508 in a palatial Italian stucco home with a sprawling old live oak tree by the driveway.

As you pass Lexington and approach Euclid you can look across the lake to the John R. Black mansion, most easily seen in winter when the trees are bare. Edgar Flippen's partner, Hugh Prather, built the home in 1917 at 4700 Preston on 7.7 acres that back up to the lake. This traditional red-brick Colonial Revival home was designed by Anton Korn.

A classical Italian Renaissance house built in 1913 stands at the corner of Euclid at 4700 Lakeside. Notice the classic green tile roof and the matching roof on the garage or carriage house. At 4704 stands a superb Colonial Revival house. Another early home was built in 1911 at 4712 Lakeside by a friend of Col. Henry Exall, Dr. Edward Cary, as a wedding gift and remained in the family for over sixty years. German craftsmen lived on the property for three years completing the fine work. The stained glass windows, possibly Tiffany's, the Spanish tile of the fountain,

13

and other details reflect the Carys' travels. This was the second home built on Lakeside.

Among the transplanted European period-style homes on Lakeside once stood an incredible Craftsman house at 4800, built in 1911, the first house on Lakeside. The Craftsman style, inspired by the Greene brothers of California, was the dominant style for smaller houses built from 1905 to the early 1920s. There are several Highland Park neighborhoods filled with these homes. This one was unusually large and grand. Unlike columns set at porch level, the supports started at ground level and went all the way up, with exposed rafters and exposed structural work. Although several historical societies tried to save the house, it was suddenly bulldozed in the fall of 1987. John D. Murchison, Jr., is building the new home. The old Craftsman carriage house and guest house on the back of the lot, being used temporarily for storage during construction, will be preserved at Old City Park, if enough money can be raised.

Col. Henry Exall and his descendants could survey the panoramic view of the lake he dammed and the area he envisioned developing from the vantage point of the home at 4808 Lakeside. Mrs. Sallie Dickson, mother of Mrs. Henry Exall, Sr., bought the house in 1916 and the Exalls began living there before 1920. Col. Exall's soft-spoken wife, May Dickson Exall, achieved distinction by being active president of the Dallas Shakespeare Club for fifty-two years, as well as by persuading philanthropist Andrew Carnegie to donate $50,000 for Dallas's library. The home's ownership passed in 1922 to her and the Exall family, who enjoyed it for many years until its sale in 1985. It has since been extensively remodeled.

The residence at 4900 Lakeside with the intricate tilework in the sidewalk was designed by Anton Korn around 1916. The Colonial Revival house at 4908 Lakeside, built in 1915 for Orville Thorpe, state manager of the Kansas City Life Insurance Company, was designed by Thomson and Fooshee. Marion Fooshee's first job as an architect, before forming his own company, was with the firm of Hal Thomson.

The estate of wealthy oilman Ed Cox at the corner of Beverly and Preston, above the limestone cliffs, was once the home of one of Highland Park's most colorful eccentrics, Rose Lloyd. Built in 1912, the lavish Italianate mansion was one of the first along the lake. Mrs. Lloyd was said to be so wealthy that when the tax budget for the newly incorporated Town of Highland Park was mistakenly sent to her home, she sat down and wrote a check for the entire amount, thinking it was her tax statement.

The stately homes and manicured lawns along Turtle Creek make this walk pleasing to the eye in every direction, as ducks and swans glide by, replacing the steamboat of a bygone era. The sidewalk leads right down to the creek where ducks are apt to scamper up for crumbs and where more than one fisherman has found his luck.

Whatever the season, a stroll along Lakeside Drive is a refreshing one, evoking memories of wild Indians and early settlers, and of men in straw hats and ladies with parasols picnicking on the shore in the serene shade that draws their grandsons and granddaughters today.

Built in 1911, the first house on Lakeside Drive, and bulldozed in October, 1987, the Harrington House at 4800 Lakeside was the grandest example in Dallas of a large Craftsman-style house. *Photo by Glenn Galloway*

4900 Lakeside

15

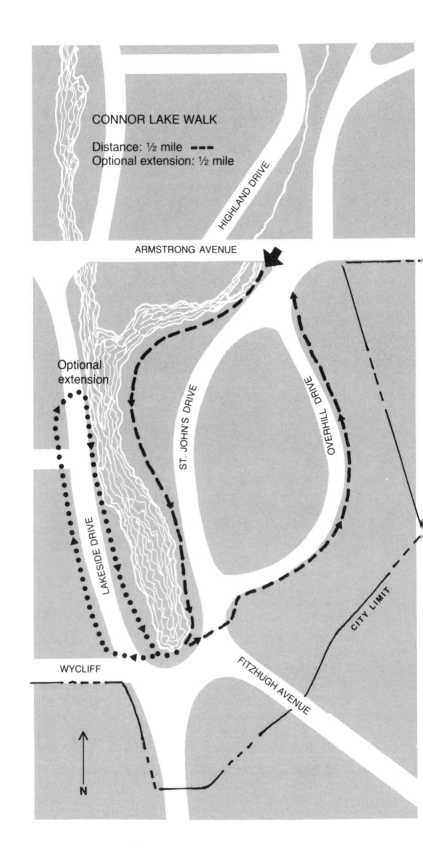

Connor Lake Walk

FIRE WAS a grim reaper of frame buildings in the early years of the Park Cities. Nearly all the first buildings on the campus of Southern Methodist University succumbed to fire. Whenever disaster struck, the fledgling fire departments of Highland Park and University Park did what they could. A tale is told of a fire on Euclid Avenue near the Highland Park Town Hall where the firefighters had spread out their hoses and were dousing a large blaze. About that time the trolley sped down the hill and, since the fire hoses were spread across the tracks, cut the hoses right in two. The firemen watched helplessly as the house burned to the ground.

The installation of modern electric and gas utilities generally brought increased safety over kerosene lanterns, open fireplaces, and woodburning stoves. Therefore it is ironic that one of the worst fires in the Park Cities, which claimed three lives near Connor Lake, was an electrical fire caused by faulty wiring in the basement.

This picturesque white frame house shown covered with snow was the scene of one of the worst fires in the Park Cities, in which three people were killed in 1951. *Courtesy of the First RepublicBank Park Cities*

Connor Lake Walk

MANY NAMES have been attached to the area—Lakeside Park, Connor Lake Park, Lake Nokomis, and, by the occasional passerby, the "glory hole" or morning-glory lake. But a rose by any other name is still a rose, and whatever you choose to call it, this is one of the most attractive lakeside areas in all of Dallas. Located where Hackberry Creek and Turtle Creek converge after traversing the length of the Park Cities, it is part of a greenbelt area that extends all the way to downtown Dallas. A proposal has been made to establish a walking trail all along this greenbelt, which would be a boon to those who enjoy getting a first-hand look at the world around them.

Put on your walking shoes and direct them toward the intersection of Armstrong and St. John's for a walk through this lovely lakeside area, past rows of historic homes and the remains of one of the worst fires in Park Cities history. There is even a hill to climb at the end.

In the wooded triangle of land created where the two creeks converge lived the second mayor of Highland Park (1914–1915), W. O. Connor, who was chairman of the board of Republic Bank. The Connors' huge eight-bedroom, eight-bath home had three stories full of nooks and crannies that visiting grandchildren delighted in exploring—the stuff from which unforgettable memories are made.

As you begin walking south from the bridge, you can get glimpses of the triangle of land across Hackberry Creek. The Connors owned the land all the way to Fitzhugh Avenue (which becomes Wycliff west of the creek) and used it as a farm—cows, chickens, and all. The path on which you are walking was once a cattle trail. There were no paved roads in sight. Mrs. Connor was an accomplished horticulturist and naturalist who planted many of the trees you see across the creek. She lived into her late nineties.

When their daughter married Frank Austin, the Connors gave her the part of the farm on which you are standing. The Austins built a three- or four-bedroom house with a tennis court, a small fishpond, and an elaborate barbecue

Highland Park Lake was one of the early names used along Turtle Creek, as shown above the gate on this old postcard published by J. T. Faber (Milwaukee), postmarked 1910. *Courtesy of the Dallas County Heritage Society at Old City Park*

19

pit by the creek. Connecting their home with the "big house" across the creek was an old bridge that their two children, Frank, Jr., and Dorothy, used to race across when they wanted to visit their grandparents.

When Dorothy Austin was a teenager this land was still "out in the country." Several young girls in the area had been molested, so the Austins installed burglar bars on all their windows and a wrought iron gate with a lock at the top of the interior stairs. After the Connors died, the Austin family moved into the "big house" across the creek and sold their home to a doctor and his wife, who bought it partly because of the burglar bars and, in fact, added two or three more bars to each window. The doctor built a terraced rose garden where the tennis court had been and planted many cherry trees that bloomed profusely in the spring. None of the cherry trees remain.

The doctor died, and in time his widow married William Flippen, brother of Edgar Flippen of Flippen-Prather Realty Company. Many years passed and by 1951 William Flippen had become an invalid. Mrs. Flippen seldom left him in the evenings, but one night she asked their maid, Edith, who had worked for Mr. Flippen for forty years, to stay in the house instead of her garage apartment while she went to a club meeting. Late that night after they were all asleep, Mrs. Flippen awoke to the choking smell of smoke. She struggled to put her husband in his wheelchair, then wheeled him to the top of the stairs, where she was unable to open the locked wrought iron gate.

Edith, who awoke downstairs, had the key and apparently tried desperately on the smoke-filled stairway to unlock the gate. Finally, succumbing to the smoke coming from the basement below, Edith fell, hitting her head on a bookcase. Frantically Mrs. Flippen wheeled her husband back to the bedroom, broke a big bay window with a chair, and collapsed. Firemen arrived on the scene but were unable to break through the burglar bars and locked gate. By the time they reached the three victims, all had died from smoke inhalation. The firemen were able to piece the story together from where the bodies lay.

Only a few months later, Armstrong School burned to the ground, but fortunately no one was injured in that blaze. The half-burned Flippen house remained on the lot for a long time, a grim reminder of the tragedy that shook the community. At the time of this writing, the land where the house burned belongs to Lamar Hunt.

Take a moment to walk around this vacant lot, which reveals the remains of the oval cement and stone fishpond, a large indentation where the basement was, and fragments of the foundation. The deteriorating barbecue pit was bulldozed in 1988. Walk to the back of the lot and look across the creek. The Creole Revival–style home, designed by Wilson McClure in 1942, was built by the Austins when they tore down the original Connor home. Lambert's Landscape did the extensive landscaping and supervised the removal of the old bridge across the creek.

Follow the path south along the creek past the curving stone retaining walls that are the remains of the terraced rose garden. A little farther south you'll see a paved area around a street lamp, with some benches nearby. The bronze marker set on a marble base says "Connor Park." The Connors willed their farm, except for the two lots where the houses stood, to the Town of Highland Park, so it is through their generosity that we can enjoy this peaceful park. Sit on a bench for a moment to enjoy the natural beauty of the area, where showy azaleas bloom in the spring. There is a strong sense of history here. Those who named this Nokomis Lake must have seen the lake during nights of the full moon, surely a magnificent sight reflecting on the water with few trees to block the view. (Nokomis means "daughter of the moon" and was the name of Hiawatha's grandmother in the poem by Henry Wadsworth Longfellow.) The frog croaking his song at dusk may be sitting on an arrowhead or pottery shard from a past Indian encampment. The mallard gliding along may be passing a spot where a dinosaur once stood. Yet the casual visitor sitting near the street lamp or fishing (with a permit) for an elusive sun perch from the calm waters of the lake may be completely unaware of the feet that have trod this sloping creek bank in the past, or of the tragedy that took place nearby.

Continue walking south along Connor Lake until you reach the giant hole that takes the water underground. When this addition of Highland Park opened in 1919, a well-known architect named Anton Korn, a new arrival to Dallas, was commissioned to build many of the homes in this scenic setting. **For an optional extension to your walk, if you care to get a close view of Korn's houses, circle around the "glory hole" and cross Lakeside Drive. (If not, simply read the next few paragraphs and continue.)**

Born in Bavaria in 1886, Anton Franz Korn established

4201 Lakeside

himself in Dallas in 1916, designing and building large, impressive residences such as the ones you see all along Turtle Creek; he built all of these between Wycliff and Armstrong. As you can see walking past the stately homes, Korn's architecture is classical, reflecting his love of nature, music, and art. He has been credited with introducing the Tudor style to the Park Cities, but he was by no means limited to one style. Each home in this section is different. He was able to take the best features of each style and, by combining those elements, give birth to his own creations.

In addition to residences, Korn designed many public buildings in Dallas, including several of the 1936 Centennial buildings at Fair Park. The old downtown YMCA has been torn down, but the Hillcrest Mausoleum, which he considered his most beautiful and enduring work, still stands. It was his choice for his final resting place when he died in 1942. Something of the quiet, deeply religious nature of the man is revealed by a fact his family learned several years after his death. During the Depression, Korn had given financial assistance to about twenty college students so they would be able to complete their studies. Yet he had told no one of these gifts.

4205 Lakeside

The generosity of men such as Korn or Connor will be seen repeatedly in the history of the Park Cities and will often be remembered in the homes they have left behind or in the fountains, plaques, and markers that bear their names.

Some of Korn's homes here on Lakeside Drive have changed owners many times since the twenties. But the gray stucco Tudor home at the corner of Wycliff and Lakeside, at 4201 Lakeside, was owned by the Charles C. Huff family for nearly seventy years. Mr. Huff was a lawyer for the Missouri-Kansas-Texas railroad (known as the "Katy"). The modified Colonial Revival home next door at 4205 Lakeside, with its unusual partial roof extending above the first-story windows, was built for T. W. Griffiths and his wife in 1917 and still remains in the family. Griffiths, one of the largest retail lumber merchants in Texas, raised seven children in this home. At 4209 you'll find two trees growing directly out of the doorstep. The house at 4211 was first owned by Henry Exall, Jr., whose father originally planned to develop this land as Philadelphia Place. (The Exall Lake Walk tells how it came to be Highland Park instead.) Don't miss the Spanish Eclectic home at 4215, with its arched windows and Roman numerals above the second-story window dating the house back to 1923.

The Tudor home across Prescott at 4301 Lakeside, with front-facing gables showing unique brickwork, stands on a large landscaped lot enclosed by a brick fence that extends across to Oak Lawn. For over ten years it belonged to Harding Lawrence, president of Braniff Airlines at the time, and his wife, advertising executive Mary Wells, whose idea it was to paint Braniff planes in a rainbow of colors. The rest of the land from here to Armstrong Avenue is owned by the Third Church of Christ Scientist Corporation.

Return to Fitzhugh (Wycliff) and round the corner past the "glory hole," where daring mallards may be standing on the edge pecking away at the algae growing on the concrete. Notice the large Neoclassical tan brick home at 4100 St. John's with its impressive two-story Ionic columns, the southernmost piece of property in Highland Park.

Cross to Overhill Drive. The hill you're about to climb can't compare in size with those of Beverly Hills in California, designed by the same land planner who laid out Highland Park, Wilbur David Cook. But the homes are equally magnificent and tasteful, flanked by stately trees that absorb the sounds of nearby traffic, creating a tranquil island neighborhood only steps away from several major arteries of Dallas.

Many of the homes that grace Overhill Drive were designed by some of the finest architects in Dallas. Anton Korn designed the two Tudor homes on the corner, at 4200 St. John's and 4302 Overhill. Fooshee and Cheek, who designed the Highland Park Village, created the gray modified Tudor with two chimneys at 4304 Overhill. As the hill rises, a pink Spanish Mediterranean with an ornate doorway appears at 4308, a home created by Hal Thomson. (For more on Hal Thomson, see the Versailles Walk.) The astounding live oak trees rival any others in the Park Cities for their grandeur. Nearby is a stunning white-trunked sycamore.

As you descend the hill on your way back to Armstrong, you'll pass a palatial white Spanish home with huge stained glass windows at 4321. At one time the Hugh Prather family lived in this home. It was designed by J. Allen Boile, who also designed the Mediterranean-style villa for cotton broker Shepherd King that was later restored as The Mansion on Turtle Creek, a hotel and restaurant. Across the street at 4348 Overhill is an extensively remodeled Fooshee and Cheek home.

Thus ends your walk of tranquility contrasted with tragedy, filled with beauty and history. Another day or another season you'll surely want to walk it again.

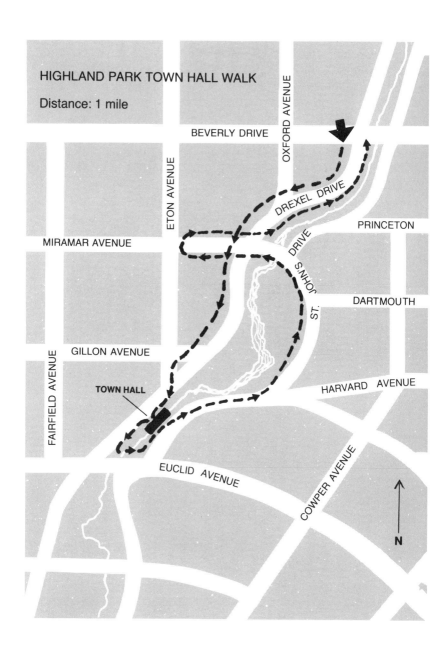

HIGHLAND PARK TOWN HALL WALK

Distance: 1 mile

OXFORD AVENUE

BEVERLY DRIVE

ETON AVENUE

DREXEL DRIVE

PRINCETON

MIRAMAR AVENUE

ST. JOHNS DRIVE

DARTMOUTH

GILLON AVENUE

FAIRFIELD AVENUE

TOWN HALL

HARVARD AVENUE

EUCLID AVENUE

COWPER AVENUE

N

Highland Park Town Hall Walk

IN THE MOOD for a mystery? Amateur sleuths need look no further than Highland Park Town Hall where, right next door to the police station, a number of valuables have strangely disappeared. The most famous disappearance was that of *Lady in Grey*, a painting by William M. Chase, the most valuable piece of Highland Park's art collection, valued at $40,000. It was stolen in 1983 and has never been recovered.

In 1937 Highland Park's art collection numbered over a hundred pieces. The current collection includes but fifty-three paintings, prints, and engravings displayed throughout Town Hall and dating from the 1800s to 1940. No one seems to know what happened to the other fifty-odd pieces as the years passed. Also missing are a bronze plaque dedicated to Mrs. A. H. Bailey, the second president of the Highland Park Society of the Arts, founded in 1924, and early memorabilia that were once displayed in a case in the upstairs hallway. To date, these mysteries remain unsolved.

Highland Park Town Hall Walk

ONE OF THE first ordinances of the Town of Highland Park prohibited residents from allowing their cattle, horses, and chickens to run at large—an early precedent to today's leash law! Times have certainly changed since the Spanish Mediterranean–style Town Hall opened its doors in 1924.

Begin your walk at the intersection of Drexel and Beverly and walk south on Drexel along beautiful Hackberry Creek. As you cross Miramar, notice the portion of the street east of Drexel, which was once part of the creek but was filled in to extend the street. Between Miramar and Gillon you can get a distant view of the Town Hall tower. Also between Miramar and Gillon, you'll pass an interesting contemporary home, designed by Enslie Oglesby, at 4808 Drexel. The house is set back from the street on the sloping lot and is reached by a footbridge.

In 1913 the citizens of Highland Park requested annexation by Dallas, but Dallas refused, a decision they would later regret. So, in that same year, Highland Park voted to incorporate (47 to 7) and elected W. A. Fraser as their first mayor (1913–1914).

Approaching Town Hall, you'll arrive at Bartholow Square, named for a former councilman. Around the Square (actually a triangle between Gillon and Eton) are three homes built by architect Hal Thomson, all in different styles. At 4726 Drexel is the home of Enslie Oglesby, the architect who designed the contemporary house you saw in the previous block, who says his home was the first Spanish Mediterranean house built in Dallas, in 1919. A classic style with Ionic columns is located at 3722 Gillon, while the home on the corner of Eton and Gillon at 3801 Gillon is an unusual Tudor-type home with a false thatched roof. (For more about Hal Thomson, see the Versailles Walk.)

The Town Hall was designed in the Spanish Mediterranean style even before that style was chosen for Highland Park Village. The ornate cream-colored structure with a red tile roof was built in the early twenties at a cost of $65,000. It was designed by Otto H. Lang, called by some the "dean of Texas architects," who with his partner, Frank Witchell, was responsible for many of Dallas's early buildings such as the YMCA and the Magnolia Building. By the time the Town Hall was built, Frank M. Smith was mayor (1924–1928).

The Highland Park Town Hall was built in 1923 in the Spanish Mediterranean style. *Courtesy of the Town of Highland Park*

Highland Park's first fire truck was a 1914 Cadillac. Notice the name of W. O. Connor, second mayor of Highland Park, on the side. The first fire station was a separate building from the Town Hall; at one time a car could drive between the two buildings. *Courtesy of the Dallas Public Library*

A conversation at lunch one day with W. A. Dealey, publisher of the *Dallas Morning News*, gave Mayor Smith an inspiration, and at the formal opening of the Town Hall on August 10, 1924, he announced an innovative plan. The rush of modern metropolitan life, he said, was causing neighbors to lose contact with each other. (Remember, this was over sixty years ago.) Therefore he had appointed a planning committee to make the Town Hall a meeting place and fine arts center with monthly art and music programs for the entire community. His goal was for the Town Hall to have one of the finest public art galleries in the country.

Before entering the Town Hall itself, take a peek at every child's favorite stop, the fire station. If the doors are open, don't miss the chance to go inside and look at the engines. The oldest dates back to 1921, and countless children have delighted in ringing its bell and imagining the wind in their faces as they rush to a fire. Each year the old fire truck graces the Park Cities Fourth of July parade at Goar Park.

In 1960 the courtroom and council chambers were added to Town Hall at a cost of $212,000, and the buildings were air-conditioned and refurbished. In 1975 the Town Hall received a $660,000 face-lift, including landscaping and bubbling fountain. The parking lot just outside the fire station was added, as well as the arched gallery that joins the Town Hall with the fire and police departments. The stucco has blended together so well, it's impossible to tell where the old ends and the new begins.

Enter Town Hall through the ornate doorway and climb the carpeted stairway to your left. As you climb the stairs, you will see one of the most famous of the paintings collected in the early days, *Betty the Gypsy Girl* by H. E. Schnakenberg. At one time it was loaned to the Dallas Museum of Art. But the most valuable piece of the art collection, William M. Chase's *Lady in Grey,* was stolen in 1983. Valued at $40,000, it was never recovered. The insurance money was used to restore some of the other paintings in the collection. The theft prompted much tighter security for the remainder of the Highland Park art collection, valued in 1983 at $80,000. The current collection contains about fifty-three paintings, prints, and engravings, dating from the 1800s to 1940, displayed throughout Town Hall.

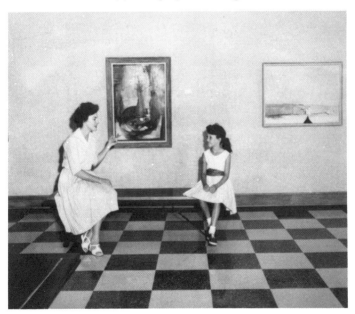

Mrs. Mary Beasley Nye and Linda Christine Linn are shown in the Highland Park Art Gallery, located in what is now the second-floor reference room of the Highland Park Library. The photo was probably taken in the early fifties. *Courtesy of the Town of Highland Park*

The courtroom and council chambers that were added in 1960 are located upstairs. Hanging in the hallway are several paintings and a collection of World War I French poster prints. The Highland Park Society of the Arts began the same year Mayor Smith envisioned it, 1924. The first president was W. A. Dealey, but soon an active member, Mrs. A. H. Bailey, took over and was the only other president the Society ever had. The Society began to collect art and held monthly community cultural meetings, providing a forum for local artists and musicians. In 1926 the Society held a "book week" to obtain books to found a library. The event kindled interest in the library, but funds were not available until a bond election passed in 1929 (60 to 55) for $75,000 to build the library and art gallery annex, which opened in 1930. In 1934 there were forty-two art pieces in their collection, valued at that time at $10,000 to $12,000, and by 1937 there were around a hundred pieces.

By the mid-fifties, TV had taken its toll and interest was waning in the Society of the Arts. Mrs. Bailey had died, and the remaining officers turned the art collection and their piano and furniture over to the town. With the remaining funds in the treasury, a bronze plaque in honor of Mrs. Bailey was placed on the wall. Its whereabouts is unknown today. The community meeting room, walnut paneled and carpeted, now contains the Society's piano and original furniture.

Return downstairs and walk back to the Louise Childress Library at the end of the hall. The library complex actually faces east on St. John's and has an entry door there as well. Louise Childress was the director until 1967, then Maxine Anderson, and in 1981 the current director, Bonnie Case, took the busy job.

As you enter the glass-paneled doors, you'll see the original curving oak reception desk, now sheathed in terracotta laminate, as are the ends of the old bookstacks, which have been retained. The dark green marble baseboards throughout the library have not been changed over the years. On your right are a bronze plaque and a painting of Louise Childress.

The children's section on the right still has the original low oak tables, but now they are covered in colorful laminate, and the chairs have been refinished. A puppet stage provides an outlet for active imaginations.

To the left of the reception desk, notice the original iron gates in the doorway leading to the adult reading room. The room still has the old classical fireplace, but the oak furniture by Stendig and Metropolitan is new, as are the 3/4-inch-thick windows that let in the sunshine but keep out the heat and cold. Here as in the upstairs reference room, which was the original art gallery, you can see pieces of art from the Society collection. Some Currier and Ives prints adorn the walls of the stairwell leading to the upstairs reference room.

As you leave the library the way you came in, notice the display case in the hall. It was once located in the second-floor hallway, where it contained old photographs and memorabilia. No one has an answer to what has become of the memorabilia in recent years, another part of the mystery of Town Hall.

The library is open Tuesday through Saturday from 9:30 to 5:30. Until 1978 anyone could check out a book free of charge. Residents can still check out books free, but in 1978 nonresident fees began. The current fee is $65 per year. The newest addition to the library is the large video tape collection begun in 1983 with a $50,000 donation by Douglass Brown. The fee to check out videos is $100 per year for nonresidents.

As you leave Town Hall, notice the cornerstone dated 1923 just south of the entrance. Among the names listed is that of Michael Costello, who in 1907 built the first house in Highland Park, now located at Old City Park. (See the Abbott Walk.)

Walk farther south for a view of the landscaping of Hackberry Creek. Then continue south to Euclid and walk across the bridge to the other side of the creek. From this side you can climb down into the charming landscaped area and can actually see the creek running under Town Hall.

Turn left on St. John's and continue north past the "front" entrance to the library. Directly across the street is an old Prairie-style home at 4700 St. John's, built possibly as early as 1910, that now houses the consulate of Monaco. The home next door at 4704 is also one of the oldest houses in the First Addition of Highland Park, built in 1912.

As you cross Harvard, keep to the left to stay on St. John's. Turn left on Miramar, crossing the creek, and continue on Miramar across Drexel. On your left at the

Consolidation of the Town of Highland Park with the City of Dallas was a controversial issue in the late 1920s.

corner of Miramar and Eton, behind the tall hedges at 3727 Miramar, is another contemporary home designed by Enslie Oglesby. Like the one we saw earlier on Drexel, it is well blended into its environment and may be hard to see from the street. You may want to walk around the corner on Eton for a better view.

Retrace your steps to Drexel, turn left, and continue north to Beverly. Don't miss the magnificent Tudor house architect Anton Korn designed for himself at 3635 Beverly, on the southwest corner of Beverly and Drexel.

Walking past these beautiful homes and parkways, you'll agree that it's no mystery why Dallas changed its mind about annexing Highland Park. Annexation became a hotly debated issue in the late twenties, splitting friendships and partnerships. By 1928 the situation had become critical. A group of wealthy Highland Park citizens even discussed buying the country club and the artesian wells that supplied the town's water in order to block annexation. But the vote went in favor of independence, and tensions eased. One more time, during World War II, the issue would come up again, but Dallas never succeeded in rectifying its mistake of 1913.

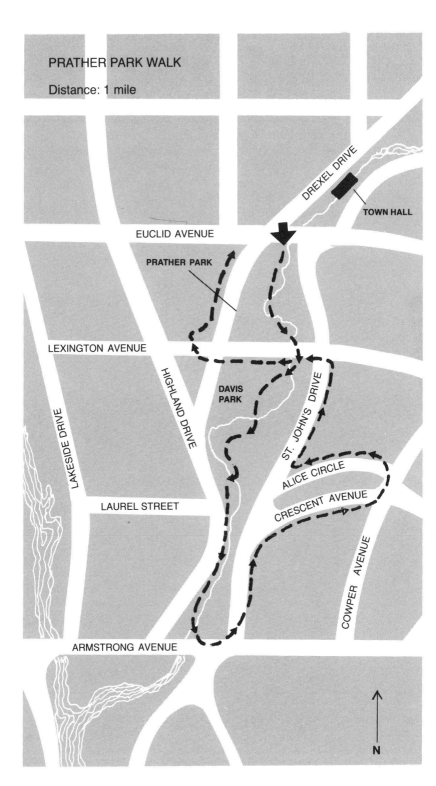

PRATHER PARK WALK

Distance: 1 mile

TOWN HALL

DREXEL DRIVE

EUCLID AVENUE

PRATHER PARK

LEXINGTON AVENUE

HIGHLAND DRIVE

DAVIS PARK

LAKESIDE DRIVE

ST. JOHN'S DRIVE

ALICE CIRCLE

CRESCENT AVENUE

LAUREL STREET

COWPER AVENUE

ARMSTRONG AVENUE

N

Prather Park Walk

JOHN ARMSTRONG, who originated the idea of a development called Highland Park, wanted to hire the best possible professional help to lay it out. So he and Hugh Prather, his son-in-law, went to Los Angeles to hire noted landscape architect Wilbur David Cook, who was then designing what today is Beverly Hills.

Cook asked if they had a topographic map, thinking that these Texans probably had never heard of such a thing. He was quite impressed when they presented him with one, and agreed to travel to Dallas to draw up the master plan for the Town of Highland Park.

From the outset Highland Park was to be an exclusive community with fine homes and lots of park land. About twenty percent of the original townsite was set aside for parks, and the town still maintains fifteen parks. Since John Armstrong died before he could carry out his plan, his two sons-in-law, Hugh Prather and Edgar Flippen, continued his work. Prather's son, Hugh Prather, Jr., still lives in Highland Park and sells real estate.

Thanks to a good original master plan, with property deed restrictions that included architectural control, Highland Park has become one of the most beautiful communities in the country, rivaling even Beverly Hills. Prather Park is just one example of the community's beauty and charm.

Prather Park Walk

CROSS A DANGEROUS drawbridge to a medieval castle
. . . swing precariously over rushing Amazon waters . . .
climb the crow's nest of your pirate's ship and check the
shore through its crude telescope. At Prather and Davis
Parks, you're limited only by your imagination, so take
along a young friend—if only young at heart—and throw
off the shackles of city life for a tour of the imagination.

You can vary your path by crossing a different bridge or
by climbing a different set of stairs. This is a walk that
changes every time you make it, no matter what the season. Springtime transports you through a wonderland of
flowers and blooming trees, and in summer the cool shade
trees create a delightful oasis. Autumn takes you on a journey through a magical forest filled with glorious fall color
and migrating birds, and even winter has its own special
charm, revealing secret shapes and spaces hidden by fo-
liage the rest of the year.

**Begin your walk at the bridge at the intersection of Eu-
clid and Drexel, just south of Highland Park Town Hall.**
Notice that the white-painted walls of the bridge were built
in 1908, the year after Mr. Costello built the first house in
Highland Park at 3500 Lexington. (See the Abbott Walk for
more about Costello.) The date can be seen on the sides of
the walls. **On either side of the south wall of the bridge
a set of steps will lead you into Prather Park. Take your
choice, and walk south along the creek.** You will pass beneath huge cedar and red oak trees. Below the limestone
cliffs of Hackberry Creek you'll see a well-protected tennis
court, especially good for windy days.

Take a look at the chalky white rock that makes up the
cliffs, which can carry you far back in time. The limestone,
characteristic of the Cretaceous period over a hundred million years ago, is made of trillions of shells of sea creatures
deposited and compressed when this area was a warm,
shallow ocean. Dinosaurs with horns and armor were
plentiful during this time. Your tour of the imagination can
begin here as you feel the ground shake and hear the deafening sound of trees crashing down around you while the
terrible *Tyrannosaurus rex* engages in a duel to the death
with his foe, *Triceratops*. This same limestone formation

The young lady seated on a bridge in Prather Park in 1927 is Sarah Chokla Gross, then a student at SMU. *Courtesy of the SMU Archives*

stretches from the Red River south through Highland Park and all the way to Austin. The presence of bentonite in the limestone indicates there was also volcanic activity in this area. Man had not yet made his appearance on the earth.

Both Hackberry Creek and Turtle Creek run the length of Highland Park. There were no lakes in the Park Cities area when the early settlers arrived. Col. Henry Exall dammed Turtle Creek at Lakeside Drive in 1890 to form what is now Exall Lake. Imagine the delight of those early pioneers at finding the natural springs that flowed nearby, after roaming the dry, parched Texas land.

Notice the old cars in the background in this photo taken at the Highland Park Pool in Davis Park in 1923. *Courtesy of the First RepublicBank Park Cities*

Climb one of the stairs at the south end of Prather Park. Across Lexington you'll see a summertime haunt of local children, who still take to the water to beat the heat—the Highland Park Pool in Davis Park.

Cross Lexington and enter Davis Park either at the stairs in the middle of the block near the pool or the stairs around the corner on St. John's. Davis Park extends from Lexington to Armstrong along meandering paths designed by Arthur and Marie Berger, both prominent landscape architects. In the forties Arthur created the original design for the DeGolyer gardens, located near White Rock Lake, which recently were updated by landscape architect Dick Myrick and became the Dallas Arboretum. Davis Park was named for H. R. Davis, mayor of Highland Park (1920–1924), but is more commonly called Drexel Park or the Highland Park Pool Park. The pool area actually used to be a rock quarry where they dug rock for streets and hauled it out with wagons and teams of horses.

41

A few of the trees bear labels high on their trunks. The old cedar elms are plentiful here, as are the hackberries and the cedars. You'll even see an occasional cherry laurel or redbud tree.

Walk around to the west side of the pool to the playground adjacent to Drexel. The playground offers that pirate's or bird's-eye view of the world from several telescopes mounted on a wooden platform. Go ahead, take a peek at Plymouth Rock from the Mayflower . . . remember the Alamo . . . land on the moon. This walk is for the explorer in your soul!

If you prefer to do your exploring in the here and now, take heart. This is one of the best spots in the Park Cities for bird watching. Early in the morning in the spring or fall your patience may be rewarded by the song of a warbler or the sight of a colorful goldfinch. Or year-round you may see a bright red cardinal, an audacious mockingbird, or even a red-bellied woodpecker. The racing feet of generations of children have provided many well-worn paths in the area of Hackberry Creek for you to roam in your search.

Just south of the swimming pool, near the swings, you'll come upon an unusual bridge. It could be a drawbridge crossing the moat of a medieval castle or a swinging bridge straddling the roaring Amazon River. **Cross the bridge and follow the path that leads to the right of the tennis court.** Notice the bronze plaque set in the ground next to the path, dated 1962, in honor of the Bergers. **Turn right again just past the tennis court, cross another bridge, and continue south toward Armstrong.** The trail closest to the creek eventually comes to a dead end, so if you go that far you'll need to backtrack and make your way up to the street to continue south. On your left you'll soon see a small meadow and a grove of magnificent old magnolia trees, reminders of antebellum ladies in hooped skirts and soldiers in Confederate uniforms, somewhere in the South.

At Armstrong, turn left and cross the bridge for a reminder of another day and time, when Indians roamed the Southwest. On the north side of each wall of the bridge is written "Nokomis." You may recall that Nokomis, which means "daughter of the moon," was Hiawatha's grandmother in Longfellow's poem "Song of Hiawatha." A 1909 plat shows the area of the lake where Hackberry Creek flows into Turtle Creek, just south of this bridge, as "Lake Nokomis." Notice the huge old American elm tree at the northeast corner of the bridge.

Turn left on St. John's and continue north. As you return past Davis Park on your way back to Euclid, you may enjoy viewing more of the beautiful old homes that grace the area. Be sure to look for the house at 4408 St. John's. It was designed by one of the founding fathers of a regional southwestern architectural style, David Williams, in collaboration with his friend O'Neil Ford. Williams considered this house his very best work. Built in 1930, it seems to blend in with its wooded, sloping surroundings—something not always considered important in the late twenties. The brick is light-colored to reflect the sun, and the roof is of standing seam copper. Notice the tall shuttered windows, the balconies, and the lattice-screened sleeping porch. Although hard to see from the street, the sturdy columns and graceful arches of the patio are reminiscent of Spanish missions of Texas. Jerry Bywaters, former director of the Dallas Museum of Art, called this exterior "architectural music." (For more on David Williams, see the Loma Linda Walk.)

Turn right and walk up Crescent toward Cowper. You'll see a small side creek rippling through the area between Crescent and Alice Circle (named for John Armstrong's wife, Alice). All of the homes nestled on this hillside blend into their environment. And where else can you find a tree growing out of the middle of the pavement?

Just before you get to Cowper, you'll see some steps on your left leading down into the area by the creek. You may want to take this shortcut and follow the path across a little stone bridge to get to Alice Circle, or you can continue to Cowper before turning left, if you prefer.

Walk back down Alice Circle toward St. John's. You'll pass two homes in a row, 3708 and 3712, designed by the versatile architect Anton Korn. (The number for 3712 may be hard to see, but the house is on the corner of Alice Circle and St. John's.) Korn's popularity as an architect in the Park Cities is evidenced by the number of homes he designed, including all the ones on the south side of the 3700 block of Beverly Drive, all on both sides of the 3300 block of Bryn Mawr, half a dozen on Potomac, all on Turtle Creek west of Connor Lake, several around the Exall Lake area, and many other showplaces.

Turn right on St. John's and continue north to Lexington, then turn left on Lexington and continue to Drexel. Notice the large marker at the corner of Lexington and Drexel, dedicated to Hugh Prather, one of Highland Park's developers, for whom Prather Park is named. Just west of the intersection at 3908 Lexington (the second house from the corner) is an indigenous-style home using local materials with an Arts and Crafts approach. Designed by O'Neil Ford, protégé of architect David Williams and partner of Arch Swank for a time, it has a modern look with a standing seam copper roof.

Continue north on Drexel to Euclid, or take a shortcut across the park, to return to your starting point at Euclid and St. John's. If contemporary homes appeal to you, a fine one designed by Enslie Oglesby can be seen south of Euclid at 4606 St. John's.

As you conclude your walk, consider a return trip in another season. The variety of trees, plants, and birds to be observed makes this an ideal nature walk for scout or school groups.

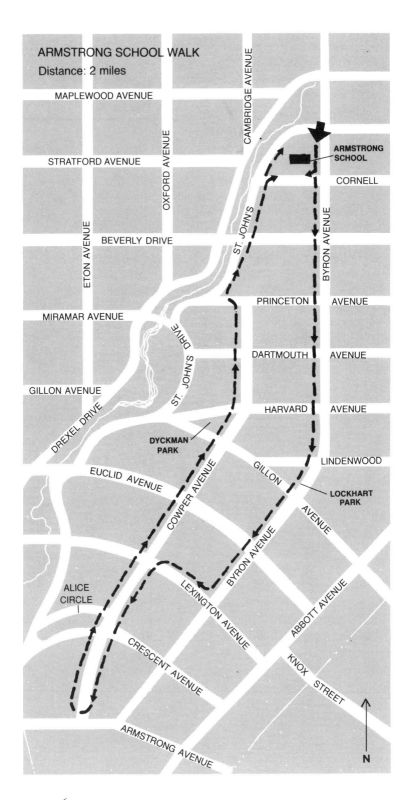

ARMSTRONG SCHOOL WALK
Distance: 2 miles

MAPLEWOOD AVENUE

STRATFORD AVENUE

ARMSTRONG SCHOOL

CORNELL

BEVERLY DRIVE

CAMBRIDGE AVENUE

OXFORD AVENUE

ETON AVENUE

ST. JOHN'S

BYRON AVENUE

PRINCETON AVENUE

MIRAMAR AVENUE

ST. JOHN'S DRIVE

DARTMOUTH AVENUE

GILLON AVENUE

HARVARD AVENUE

DREXEL DRIVE

DYCKMAN PARK

LINDENWOOD

EUCLID AVENUE

COWPER AVENUE

GILLON

LOCKHART PARK

ALICE CIRCLE

LEXINGTON AVENUE

BYRON AVENUE

AVENUE

ABBOTT AVENUE

CRESCENT AVENUE

KNOX STREET

ARMSTRONG AVENUE

N

5
Armstrong School Walk

Slowly but surely a raw bunch of boys, inexperienced but
interested in the games, has become the personnel of this
year's teams, of which we claim a right to be proud. The
Highlanders have "come from behind" in the sense that the
name "Highland Park" now strikes fear to the hearts of op-
posing teams . . . to Coach H. B. Howard is due the credit
of taking the initial step towards making athletics amount
to something for Highland Park. . . . Of no less importance
are the girls' athletics . . . two classes are held in the gym-
nasium each day at the seventh and eighth periods and
Miss Cushman makes these so interesting that almost every
girl is glad when the time comes for her to lay down her
books and refresh herself by participating in the invigorat-
ing exercises and dances.

—1924 *Highlander,* Highland Park
High School's yearbook

SPORTS HAVE LONG been a major force in
Highland Park schools, from kindergarten on up. The
action begins with the bright-eyed five-year-olds who
don uniforms bearing their school colors and learn
the basics of soccer with a size-3 soccer ball. Most any
weekday afternoon or Saturday morning the parks
and playing fields are filled with pint-sized players,
growing their way through various sports sponsored
by the Park Cities/North Dallas YMCA.

But it's at the high school level that the real excite-
ment lies, as the Scots vie on fall Friday nights for a
chance to go to the state football championship finals. The team has made the trip several times, with
the yellow-ribbon-tied-around-trees backing of their
adoring fans, the Park Cities community. In basketball season, fans of that sport fill the bleachers in Highland Park's gym, and baseball, soccer, and other sports
claim their own diehard fans throughout the year.

47

Armstrong School Walk

CERTAIN FAMILIES in the history of the Park Cities will be remembered for their far-reaching influence, such as the Caruth family who owned and developed most of the land that is now University Park and donated many acres of land so that Southern Methodist University could be located in Dallas. The Armstrong family will be remembered not only for founding Highland Park, but also for their part in the establishment of SMU and the Highland Park Independent School District (HPISD).

John Scarbrough Armstrong had a great dream, to establish the most exclusive residential community in Dallas. He wanted the finest homes and most elite homeowners, a development filled with parks and parkways, an exclusive country club, and fine schools. It would be the state's first totally planned park city. Armstrong died April 26, 1908, leaving the realization of his dream to his sons-in-law, Edgar Flippen and Hugh Prather.

Armstrong had always been interested in furthering education. In 1907 he offered a hundred acres from what is now Highland Park West to establish a Presbyterian university in Dallas, but that university never materialized. In 1911 his widow donated the hundred acres that started the SMU campus.

Highland Park grew faster than anyone's expectations, and in 1914 the newly incorporated town petitioned the Dallas County Judge to allow them to establish the HPISD. Until this time, school had been held in a frame house that had been moved to the 4700 block of Abbott by community leader Michael Costello and a group of citizens. When the school district election was held and trustees were selected, they began searching for a suitable location for their new school. Mrs. Armstrong generously donated the needed land in the area bounded by Cornell, Byron, and St. John's, in memory of her late husband, thus helping to found the HPISD and its first school, appropriately named Armstrong.

Begin your walk at the intersection of St. John's and Byron. Byron is closed to traffic between St. John's and Cornell during school hours. As you stand at the corner of the school grounds, imagine a one-story yellow brick building

The girls in Miss Cushman's seventh period gym class, participating in "invigorating exercises and dances," are photographed for the 1924 *Highlander*, the Highland Park yearbook. *Courtesy of Highland Park High School*

Some of the members of the Scots football team that were said to "strike fear in the hearts of opponents" are photographed for the 1924 *Highlander. Courtesy of Highland Park High School*

with only four rooms and a basement. This first unit of Armstrong School opened in September of 1914 with a principal and two teachers. The fourth room was not needed, so it was originally used as a Sunday-school room.

By 1916 there were twelve teachers, most without college degrees. The students, ranging from kindergarteners to seven high school sophomores, were delighted that a second floor was added that year. During this time students who wanted to complete high school had to go to Bryan Street High School in Dallas (originally called Dallas High School and later Crozier Tech). But in 1922 the addition of a high school to the system temporarily relieved the overcrowded school. The eighth and ninth graders moved into the new building, which is now Arch H. McCulloch Middle School, and in 1924 the first class graduated.

Walk south on Byron to Cornell. As Highland Park grew, Armstrong School grew. In 1924 a north wing was added, completing the H formation of the old building, and special art, music, and playground teachers were hired. Still later a gymnasium was built. But more pupils soon made more schools necessary. Armstrong can be called the alma mater of the school district, for as Bradfield (1926) and University Park (1928) were added, both teachers and pupils were drawn from Armstrong. In 1937 a new Highland Park High School opened on Emerson, with a quotation above the door that says, "Enter to learn, go forth to serve."

The first Armstrong School building housed the entire Highland Park school district from 1914 to 1922. This photo was taken in 1923 after the second floor had been added in 1916. *Courtesy of the John S. Armstrong Elementary School Library*

In 1949 Hyer School was built, completing the system, and in 1951 a new administration building opened.

That same year, 1951, a fire destroyed the original Armstrong School building, and Superintendent Buell Irvin risked personal harm to get the District's tax records out of the burning building. For two years classes met in the Highland Park Methodist Church until the new school was dedicated on the original site donated by Mrs. Armstrong. A new portrait of Mr. Armstrong was hung at that time. The school was rebuilt in the "modern" fifties style instead of the original design.

Round the corner at Cornell and walk up to the school building to read the bronze marker by the door. Just across Cornell from Armstrong School are two houses that have received plaques from the Park Cities Historical Society for their architectural significance. The house at 3607 Cornell was designed by Marion Fooshee in the Eclectic Tudor style and was built in 1923 or 1924. The steeply pitched roof, tall narrow windows, prominent cross gables, and brick wall cladding are typical Tudor features. The neighboring Eclectic Tudor home at 3615 was designed by the same architect or by his partner, James Cheek, and was built in the same year. Of particular interest are the random-stacked fieldstone, the two-story gable sweeping down to the left, the windows with diamond-shaped panes, and the three chimneys. In later years, Fooshee and Cheek designed the Highland Park Village.

Return to Byron and continue south. Imagine that most of the land around you is unplowed fields. The first homes in Highland Park were located on Lexington near Abbott, which is a pleasant walk from the school today on paved sidewalks passing well-manicured homes. But Armstrong's first students walked across open fields, some coming from as far away as the homes that had sprung up near SMU, around University and Haynie. Many children walked several miles for the privilege of going to school. One early resident remembers the crunch of all the acorns under their feet as they walked to school under the many oak trees that once lined Byron.

Cross Beverly Drive and continue south for several blocks. Begin to notice the Klein Brothers markers on the corners in the concrete. Undated sidewalks indicate that the concrete work was probably done before 1920, when Klein Brothers apparently began dating their work.

The naming of streets in Highland Park was an Armstrong family game. In the early days several neighboring families would sit at the Armstrong home on Ross Avenue poring over blueprints and musing over possible names. Son-in-law Hugh Prather suggested the names of the Ivy League schools, such as Princeton, Dartmouth, and Harvard. You'll pass these streets in that order. St. John's was named for the biblical St. John; Byron, the street on which you are walking, was named for the poet; and Euclid was a famous Greek. Edmondson was named for Hugh Prather's mother, Anne Edmondson, whose father once hid from Indians near what is now Exall Lake. Mrs. Henry Exall had already named Mockingbird Lane because of all the birds and Lovers Lane because it was a meandering, dark lane lined with bois d'arc hedges where lovers used to enjoy evening buggy rides.

And the town of Highland Park itself got its name from Henry Exall's horse farm, Lomo Alto, which meant "high hill." Just as Exall had envisioned for Philadelphia Place, Armstrong also wanted his development to be full of parks, so he named it "Highland Park." The first advertisements for Highland Park claimed the area was "beyond the city's dust and smoke." This slogan was soon replaced with "It's ten degrees cooler in Highland Park." After all, it was 130 feet higher than Dallas!

On your right you'll be approaching a park between Lindenwood and Gillon. Part of the nearly sixty acres of parks in Highland Park alone, Lockhart Park was named for James E. Lockhart, a Highland Park alderman who lived nearby in the early twenties. A bronze marker in his honor is on the west end of the park. Many small parks in Highland Park have been named for civic leaders who lived nearby. Note the date on the park sidewalk, 1921. The half-inch pigmented concrete veneer was added for cosmetic purposes.

Even though there is a newly built home on the southwest corner of Gillon and Byron, as you cross Gillon you are now entering the oldest section of Highland Park, listed in Dallas County records as the First Addition. The first lots sold in 1907 were in the area bounded by Gillon, Abbott, Armstrong, and Drexel because it was closest to public transportation, the trolley that stopped at Knox Street. This neighborhood is the heart of the exclusive community envisioned by Armstrong. (See the Old Highland Park Walk for a discussion of some of the first homes here.)

In the midst of the elite society able to afford the luxuries of Highland Park, an infamous house once stood on the northwest corner of Euclid and Byron, at 3600 Euclid. During the 1930s a gigantic whiskey factory was seized right here in the heart of Highland Park, just three blocks from the police station. The second floor was a working distillery with huge vats, capable of producing five hundred gallons per day. It took three days to dismantle the factory and dump the contents into the gutter. Rumor had it that local citizens sent their servants by night to fill up bottles, and the entire neighborhood smelled for weeks.

In fact, the thirties was a time of real challenge to the Highland Park police. The Depression caused many people from the North who were down on their luck to hop on trains and head south. Highland Park citizens certainly didn't want them in their exclusive community so they hit upon a unique solution. Just as fast as the tramps would get off the train at Knox Street, the Highland Park police would pick them up and take them to the city limits of Dallas!

The first three houses in Highland Park, including the Costello house and the Prather house, were built in the 3500 block of Lexington, near the trolley on Knox. Costello's Prairie-style home was moved to Old City Park (1717 Gano) as a Sesquicentennial project, and the Prather house has been torn down.

Turn right on Lexington. The home at 3605 Lexington may be the oldest house still standing in the Park Cities. Built in 1908, it has front-facing gables and decorative beams under the roof that indicate Craftsman influence.

When Highland Park opened in 1907 few people owned cars. An exception was Mrs. Henry Exall's brother, Joe Dickson, who owned car 376, which meant that he was the three hundred and seventy-sixth person in Dallas to own a car. But while there were few cars, many people owned horses. Just after you pass 3608 Lexington notice the original hitching ring attached to the curb. And directly across the street were more rings used to tie up horses while calling on friends. You have already passed by another one. Did you spot it? (It was in the curb on the northeast corner of Lexington and Byron.)

Turn left on Cowper and continue south to Armstrong

This 1914 photograph of the very early Prairie-style home at 3700 Armstrong shows the fence around the yard to keep the cattle out. The original wooden columns seen here have been replaced by metal ones. *Courtesy of the Dallas Public Library*

Avenue, named for Highland Park's founder. You'll pass Alice Circle, named for John Armstrong's wife, Alice. When Highland Park West was opened, Armstrong Avenue was extended there as Armstrong Parkway.

As you approach Armstrong, you'll see on the west side of Cowper the wire-fenced backyard of a very early Prairie-style home at 3700 Armstrong. On the front porch, the original wooden columns typical of Prairie-style homes have been replaced by metal ones. The house was completed in 1908 or 1909, but no one seems to remember whether it was built by John Armstrong, whose wife sold the property after his death in 1908, or by Alex W. Coke, who then bought the property and lived there with his family for many years. Since a fire destroyed many of the records at the Highland Park Town Hall in 1928, some questions have remained unanswered. Coke was a prominent lawyer whose son became the attorney for the First National Bank.

In 1936 the W. D. Prince family moved into the home, which then became the site of many parties and weddings as they raised four daughters and a son there. All of them later attended SMU. One of the Prince daughters, Marty Nichols, remembers that the Highland Park Pharmacy would deliver Cokes and chocolate Dr Peppers to the parties, much to the delight of the young crowd. Of the many sycamore trees the Princes planted around the lot only one remains, standing white-trunked and alone on Armstrong.

For your return walk, go north on Cowper to Princeton, savoring the stately homes and landscaping. Some of the trees have been there so long they have nearly outgrown their parkways. **Between Gillon and Harvard you'll pass Dyckman Park,** with a bronze marker on the west end dedicated to civic leader W. A. Dyckman (1876–1948). The park has the same kind of sidewalk as Lockhart Park. **At Princeton turn left, then right on St. John's, and enjoy following Hackberry Creek back to Armstrong School.**

The developer's influence on the quality of life and lifestyle was much more significant in the days before traffic patterns and shopping malls and zoning ordinances dictated a community's growth. From the outset Armstrong dreamed of creating the finest, most beautiful, most exclusive community in Dallas. And there are many who believe his dream is a reality. The Armstrongs left a wide-ranging legacy of parklands, gracious living, and fine schools from which today's citizens still benefit.

Abbott Walk

AT THE TURN of the century the railroad was a small town's window to the world. The train station witnessed the human drama unfolding in the lives of everyday people: partings and reunions, sons and daughters going off to college, young people leaving home to seek their fortunes and see the world, the wealthy gathering their families and leaving the Texas heat for summers in the East and North. When you traveled great distances, you went by rail, and for Highland Park that meant you left from the Knox Street station.

This photo taken from Knox Street just east of Abbott, facing northeast, shows the Highland Park Katy Railroad Station in the distance. *Photo by Roland Peterson, courtesy of the Fikes Hall of Special Collections and the DeGolyer Library, SMU*

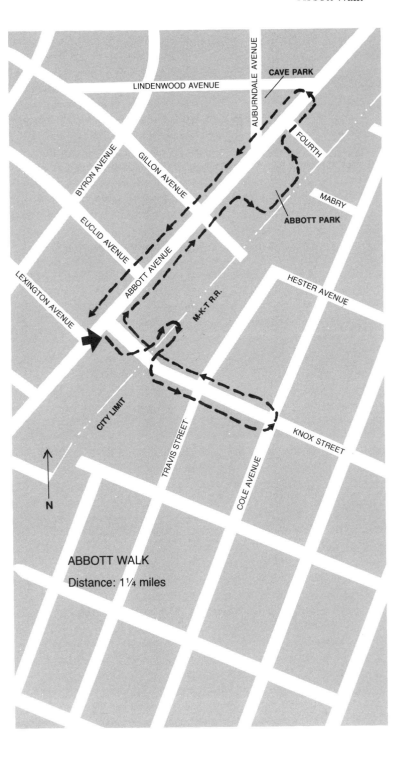

ABBOTT WALK

Distance: 1¼ miles

Abbott Walk

BEGIN your walk at the intersection of Knox Street and Abbott and walk east on Knox to the railroad tracks. When the Missouri-Kansas-Texas (MKT or "Katy") Railroad Station opened in 1922, its slogan was "Highland Park has no steps to climb"—unlike Dallas's Union Station. The Highland Park station stood north of Knox on the west side of the tracks. Walk around this area to see what remains of the station, the concrete that paved the station's platform area and some concrete squares containing metal that was part of the long, one-story brick building with a tile roof. For more than twenty years L. C. Wakefield and his brother Frank ran the small station, which at Christmastime was decorated with strings of colored lights draped across the outside walls and roof. It was the most popular station on the Katy rails.

West of the station toward Abbott was a well-kept parkway landscaped with flowers and shrubs, which extended south to Knox and north to the platform's end. Along the platform, about fourteen feet from the main-line track, were wooden benches spaced at intervals.

Passengers often rode the trolley or "Dinkey" to Knox Street, got off for a soda at the Highland Park Pharmacy (still in business today), and then caught the train at the station. When the football team of Southern Methodist University departed to meet a distant foe, fans held a grand celebration complete with a band to send them off.

The old trains transported many Highland Park graduates off to college as youngsters and brought them back as men and women. Students enrolling at SMU would arrive here. Train watching was a popular pastime for Park Cities residents. Adults and children alike waved as the Bluebonnet, the Texas Special, and the Katy Flyer sped by. A popular birthday party was an excursion to Greenville about fifty miles away. The birthday crowd would board the train at the Knox Street station, feast on cake and ice cream on the train, get off at Greenville, and wait for the next train back.

Cross the railroad tracks and walk east on Knox, leaving Highland Park. Highland Park had few businesses, so its citizens often came to the ones on Knox Street. Some Highland Park landmarks are actually located in the city

The Highland Park Pharmacy on Knox Street offered curb service back in the 1920s. *Courtesy of the Dallas Public Library*

limits of Dallas, such as Highland Park Pharmacy, built in 1912 before Knox Street was paved. The original pharmacy, founded by H. S. Forman from Tyler, was located at the northwest corner of Travis and Knox, just across from the current structure built in 1922. It was a popular hangout for lunch or a date, offering curb service in the 1920s, long before the drive-ins and carhops of the fifties. **Continue to Travis and Knox to get a better view.**

Highland Park residents also came to Knox Street to the local barber shop or to see a movie at the now defunct Knox Theater. Boarded and vacant, the old building with the painted facade still stands across from the pharmacy.

In the concrete on the corner in front of the pharmacy,

Weir's Furniture Village on Knox Street had only a twenty-foot storefront when it was founded in 1948. *Courtesy of Weir's Furniture Village*

notice the name Klein Brothers, 1923. Throughout the Park Cities, if you have a sharp eye, you'll see imprints with dates of their concrete work that give a clue to the history of the area. Although the curb is crumbling in places, the sidewalk is in remarkable shape for being over sixty-five years old.

Just east of the pharmacy was a one-room lending library where, for three cents a day, you could check out the book of your choice. Next to the pharmacy today is Weir's Furniture Village, founded in 1948 by J. Ray Weir and his wife, Bea, who sold everything from portable fans to dining room furniture. The front door is in the same location as when it was originally called Weir's Early American Shop and had only a twenty-foot storefront. The neighboring five-and-dime, post office, and lending library also had twenty-foot storefronts, which Weir took over as the years passed. The store, now run by the Weirs' son, Dan, still offers a country flavor, reminiscent of earlier days, with its Country Store in back.

Farther east, at the corner of Cole and Knox, is the Highland Park Cafeteria, another Highland Park landmark located in Dallas. As a matter of fact, neither Highland Park Presbyterian Church nor Highland Park High School, and only part of Highland Park United Methodist Church, is located in Highland Park!

Walk back to the railroad tracks. The trolley from downtown Dallas made a last stop here after its trip up Cole Avenue. When the trolley was first extended into Highland Park, it made a right on Abbott, headed west on Euclid to Highland, then north to Beverly and Fairfield and back again. Later a smaller, independently run trolley line was added which simply ran along Abbott and went up the middle of Hillcrest past SMU to University and back. The route the "Dinkey" followed eventually became the main streetcar line.

Turn right on Abbott and follow the route of the Dinkey north toward Hillcrest. You'll see many old hackberry trees, some sycamores, and even a catalpa and a maple. **As you cross Gillon, you'll see Abbott Park on your right.** Dr. Frank Abbott was a classical scholar admired by Alice Armstrong, who named the street. (See the Armstrong School Walk for more about the Armstrong family and the naming of Highland Park streets.) In 1971 a Miss Vines living at 4816 Abbott virtually gave her house to Grassroots, Inc., a black-activist group modeled after the Black Panthers. A later attempt to change the zoning so that apartments could be built here was forestalled by a petition by neighbors. The Town of Highland Park did a survey which indicated a play park was needed on the east side of the town. The town then purchased the Vines house and several other very old houses for about $26,000 each and in 1975 created picturesque Abbott Park, which you are entering. The huge old elm, pecan, and hackberry trees had been in the backyards of the homes that were torn down, and even an old apple tree remains near the back fence. The shade created by all the trees makes this a cool destination for a summer outing.

Turn right into the park and walk until you can see the old Highland Park water tower, which stands nearby. When first built, the tower was a constant irritant to the neighbors because children used to climb up the spiral ladder and bombard neighboring fences and property with rocks.

The children were not the only ones who got into trouble for climbing the water tower. In 1978 a man was charged

Children of early settlers in what is now Highland Park attended classes in the little red schoolhouse located near the water tower.

with criminal trespass for the same deed. His punishment, set by Highland Park Judge Pat Robertson, was to gather information about the tower. The man found that the tower had been built in 1924 by the Chicago Bridge and Iron Works and that its pieces were joined together with hot rivets, as welding was rare in the twenties. Beneath the 142-foot tower was an artesian well that was the central water supply for Highland Park until the thirties. In 1947 a water district was created for the Park Cities, the artesian well was capped, and the original 75,000-gallon tank was replaced by the one you see, which holds up to 250,000 gallons of water pumped by the Park Cities Water Department all the way from Lake Grapevine.

Almost as important as its utilities to Highland Park's early citizens was the establishment of the first little red schoolhouse, which was located near the water tower. Michael Costello, who built the first home in Highland

This photograph of pupils at the school was taken in 1909. *Courtesy of the John S. Armstrong Elementary School Library*

Park, led a group of residents in purchasing a frame house and moving it from McKinney Avenue to this area. Three of Costello's children promptly enrolled, as well as Hugh Prather's son John. In 1914 the new Armstrong School opened on St. John's at Byron.

Follow the winding sidewalk through the park to enjoy the trees and landscaping. Just past the park at 4822 Abbott is a home that is always colorfully landscaped with seasonal flowers. The charming yellow cottage was built on bois d'arc posts in 1914 in the eclectic Prairie style that characterized early Highland Park. Prairie-style homes such as those of architect Frank Lloyd Wright were considered the first genuinely American architecture that did not imitate past styles. The home in front of you was built during the years of the Prairie School's greatest success, 1909–1914, at a cost of $3,500. Although the architect is unknown, it has received recognition as a historic landmark and a plaque from the Park Cities Historical Society, which you can see on the front of the house.

Cross the street and return south down Abbott. You'll pass Cave Park, dedicated in 1924 to Dr. Harrison Cave, an early resident active in civic affairs who lived across the street during the time when the Dinkey traveled down Abbott. For many years a U-shaped pipe held the sign naming Cave Park, but in 1985 a new bronze plaque was donated by Dr. Cave's son, Harrison, who remembers the triangular park across from his homestead at 4820 Abbott (now torn down) and also remembers climbing the old water tower when he was about four years old. The memory of his rescue by the Highland Park Fire Department was so vivid that Cave never climbed the tower again.

At Gillon and Abbott, a tall flagpole set back from the corner marks all that is left of the first commercial structure in Highland Park, an office building built in 1911, which housed the Republic Insurance Company. This lot was originally bought from John Armstrong for $1,500.

Near the northwest corner of Euclid and Abbott there is an imprint in the concrete that says Klein Brothers, 1924. Can you find it? It's nearly worn away.

On the northeast corner of Knox and Abbott once stood a private school founded in 1913 as the Highland Park Academy. By 1920 it was popularly known as "Mrs. Morgan's School."

The vacant lot at the corner of Abbott and Lexington was the location of the first home in Highland Park, the Costello house. Behind the house was a big vegetable garden and a two-story barn for horses, cows, chickens, and geese. Eight Costello children grew up and attended school here. Michael Costello, who came to Dallas in 1888 as road superintendent for the Houston and Texas Central Railway, built his home in 1907. The 4,000-square-foot frame house, designed by H. A. Overbeck, was built in a transitional architectural style between Victorian and Prairie. The house had full-length two-story framing studs, ten-and-one-half-foot ceilings, front and back stairways, and fireplaces in the parlor and the dining room. Through the dedication of citizens unwilling to see it torn down, this landmark was carefully moved in 1986 to Old City Park (1717 Gano), where it is known as the "Park Cities Heritage House." The project coincided with the celebration of the Texas Sesquicentennial, 150 years after the Republic of Texas declared its independence from Mexico.

Michael Costello is memorable not only because of his home but also because of his spirit of volunteerism. Besides helping to found Highland Park's first school and becoming in 1914 one of the first members of the new school board, he served as unofficial (and unpaid) secretary of the Town of Highland Park for five years before he became its official secretary. He also served the town as fire marshal. The volunteer spirit that Costello exemplified still characterizes the citizens of the Park Cities and their work in the community, churches, and schools.

Cross Abbott to return to your starting point, near the place where the old Katy Railroad Station once stood—Highland Park's window to the world. The station was closed in 1968, marking the end of an era. The sound of a train whistle now is only that of an occasional freight passing through.

Old Highland Park Walk

FRONT PORCHES were gathering places in Highland Park in the early years. The John McPolan family moved to Highland Park in 1929, and at ninety Mrs. McPolan recalls many a Sunday afternoon visiting with neighbors on the porch. "We always had plenty of chairs out," she recalls, "and people would come and sit and talk." The Depression may have put a damper on many aspects of life, but perhaps in some ways it brought neighbors and families closer.

Mrs. McPolan and her neighbors shopped in Oak Lawn in those days, before the Village opened in Highland Park West. She remembers going to the A&P and the bakery there, and once, the family bulldog went to the store all by himself and returned with a steak in his mouth, lifted from the basket of some unsuspecting shopper.

A few years later, Mrs. McPolan saw dramatic evidence of the security of living in a neighborly community like Highland Park when her son left his bike parked at the Village Theatre for a week. He returned the following Saturday and there it was, unlocked and untouched. "You knew all your neighbors," said Mrs. McPolan, "and you felt safe."

That kind of security was what Highland Park's founders had in mind when they had these words engraved on a plaque outside the Town Hall: "A haven for home and fireside—undisturbed by conflict of commercial or political interests. The function of government in Highland Park is protection of the home.

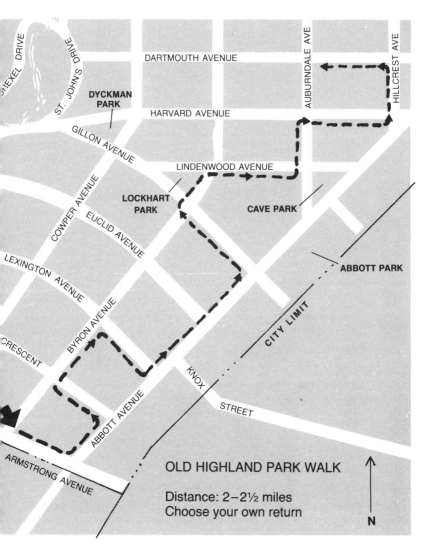

DARTMOUTH AVENUE

AUBURNDALE AVE

HILLCREST AVE

DREXEL DRIVE

ST. JOHN'S DRIVE

DYCKMAN PARK

HARVARD AVENUE

GILLON AVENUE

LINDENWOOD AVENUE

LOCKHART PARK

CAVE PARK

COWPER AVENUE

EUCLID AVENUE

ABBOTT PARK

LEXINGTON AVENUE

CITY LIMIT

BYRON AVENUE

CRESCENT

KNOX

ABBOTT AVENUE

STREET

OLD HIGHLAND PARK WALK

ARMSTRONG AVENUE

Distance: 2–2½ miles
Choose your own return

N

Citizens who cherish their homes will vigilantly preserve their heritage of self government."

The idea of home as a haven for family and friends
was instilled in the hearts of succeeding generations,
many of whom still make their homes in "Old Highland Park."

Old Highland Park Walk

IF YOU LIKE to look at older homes, this walk's for you. It's a tour of the oldest section of Highland Park, giving you a glimpse of house designs rarely found in other areas of the Park Cities.

Fashions in home styles change, just as clothing fashions change. Pattern books and popular magazines of the different eras illustrate the ebb and flow of styles. If you know what style was popular during a particular era, you can often tell by looking at a neighborhood approximately when the homes were built.

For more than a century after winning political independence from England, America was considered an artistic colony of Europe, and houses built in the United States were imitations of European styles. At the dawn of the twentieth century, however, a revolution was occurring in American architecture. American architects began turning their backs on past forms of design and decoration. They began to search for a purely American style, looking carefully at country homes, rustic cabins, and adobe structures and moving closer to nature and natural materials for their inspiration. American artists were discovering their own native style as well, as Thomas Eakins and Winslow Homer began painting scenes from American outdoor life.

The Arts and Crafts Movement, as this search for an indigenous American style was called, produced two distinctive forms of architecture. The first was the Prairie style, which began in Chicago under the leadership of a man of genius, Frank Lloyd Wright. The group of architects working with him was called the Prairie School. The second was the Craftsman style, begun in southern California by the Greene brothers. Both styles were popular from about 1905 to 1915, the Craftsman lasting a bit longer (until about 1920), but both were short-lived and by the end of World War I were out of vogue. Since Highland Park development began during this period, with its First Addition opening in the spring of 1907, the earliest neighborhoods provide a unique opportunity to see styles that were built for only a short period.

Let your walking shoes take you to 3600 Armstrong, on the west side of the intersection of Byron and Armstrong.

This is an example of a Prairie-style home, with strong horizontal interest reflecting the wide, flat expanses of the prairie on which it was built. Notice the contrasting caps on the tops of the porch and columns, and the horizontal siding, emphasizing the expansive character of the structure. The low-pitched gabled roof has widely overhanging enclosed eaves. Typical is the two-story house with a single-story porch supported by massive square columns. The porch on many Prairie houses is full width or even wraparound, but on others it is set to the side. Most of the examples of the Prairie style on this walk are high-style forms where the porch, instead of being subordinate to the two-story mass, is equally dominant.

Head east on Armstrong and you'll see another Prairie-style home at 3504 Armstrong. The characteristic horizontal emphasis is again found in the wood siding, this time with a more typical hipped roof. As you become adept at recognizing the style, you may find your own particular favorites as you walk along.

Turn left on Abbott and left again on Crescent. Notice 3504 Crescent, a cottage one might expect to find while wandering down an English country lane. Its Tudor detailing is from another era, with a wrapped roof like the thatched roofs that shed water in rainy England. In contrast, the house across the street at 3507, with its unusual shake shingle siding, exhibits variations of the Prairie style. The wide carport with hipped roof extends the horizontal lines. At 3508 is a home built in 1913, the year Highland Park was incorporated. The wraparound porch at 3515 seems to invite you to stop by for a visit to enjoy the cool evening breezes along with some conversation. The overhanging eaves are typically enclosed. The characteristic broad flat chimneys have no sign of the chimney pots that are typical of the Tudor style. This is a street of contrasts, for the house at 3512 is Spanish.

Turn right on Byron and walk north one block to Lexington. This was the first street developed in Highland Park, close to the nearest transportation, the Knox Street trolley. The first three homes to be built are gone, but one of them, the Costello house (formerly at 3500 at the east end of this block) has been preserved at Old City Park. (More about the Costello house when we pass the vacant lot where it stood.)

Another of the first three homes, formerly located on the

In 1907 or 1908 developer Hugh Prather built this home, one of the first three in Highland Park, at the corner of Lexington and Byron. The fence around the Craftsman-style house kept roaming cattle out of their yard. Prather and his family lived here until 1917 when they moved to 4700 Preston. *Courtesy of the Dallas Public Library*

southeast corner of Lexington and Byron, belonged to Hugh Prather, one of the developers of Highland Park. His sons, John and Hugh, Jr., had a little white billy goat and a little green wagon with red wheels and harness. Costello's son John would help the young Prathers hitch up the goat so they could ride around in the wagon.

Across the street on the northeast corner, at 3516 Lexington, remains a brick home with multiple hipped roofs and nicely detailed columns, built in 1914 when the popularity of the Prairie style was waning. By then the famous Prairie School architects no longer had people waiting in line for their services. They had to examine their options, which were far from satisfactory. Even the renowned Frank Lloyd Wright himself finally succumbed to bankruptcy. Another apparently committed suicide, one retired early, and others yielded to social and financial pressure and built what the public demanded. Fortunes took a favorable turn for Wright in the mid-thirties when a Wright renaissance took place, culminating in the fifties in his famed design of the Guggenheim Museum in New York City.

Not until ranch-style houses became dominant in the fifties and sixties would the characteristic horizontal look be seen again, this time in a more rambling style with low-pitched roofs. Post–World War I brought a renewed interest in period-style houses, which predominate on Lakeside Drive and in Highland Park West and Volk Estates. After World War II this trend was reversed and interest shifted back to the more "modern" styles which can be found in abundance in the postwar development north of Southwestern Boulevard in University Park. There you'll find examples of ranch-style homes with porches facing the backyards instead of the front, and split-level homes. The more austere contemporary and international styles, with their absence of all non-functional decoration, have never been popular in the Park Cities.

Walk east on Lexington toward Abbott. Take note of the open porch on the house at 3508 Lexington; most of the Prairie porches you have seen have been partially enclosed with railings. Across the street, the house at 3505 was built around 1908 but appears newer because it has been kept in good repair and the landscaping has been updated. It has

At the turn of the century young children enjoyed hitching up their pet goat to a wagon for a ride, as shown on this old postcard. The Prather children had a white billy goat and a little green wagon. *Courtesy of the Dallas County Heritage Society at Old City Park*

Another Nuisance Dispensed
with by the
GAS STOVE.
GAS CO., 561 MAIN STREET.
Telephone 241.

You will avoid this if y
use a
GAS STOVE.
Full particulars at the (
Office,
261 Main St.   Telephone

Most Physicians Will Tell You

THAT it is wiser to sleep in an unheated room. But getting up in the cold of a morning is pretty cheerless.

A GAS HEATER in your bed room will enable you to heat your room in a few minutes without even leaving your luxurious couch.

Don't dress in the cold!

"It always is there when it's wanted and never is there when it ain't."

That is why GAS is cheapest for heating.

There is

ABSOLUTELY

no waste.

thirteen-foot ceilings and red pine millwork. You see no chimneys because it has no woodburning fireplaces. The first owners used gas heaters instead, a status symbol in the early 1900s.

The vacant lot at 3500 Lexington, at the corner of Abbott, was the location of the Costello home, which has been moved to Old City Park. Although Victorian houses like those found on Swiss Avenue were out of vogue, the Costello house was built in 1907 in a transitional style between Victorian and Prairie. It was designed by H. A. Overbeck. It's worth a trip to Old City Park (located just south of downtown Dallas at 1717 Gano) to see this as well as other landmark homes on display in a small-town setting complete with its own railroad station, bank, and steepled church.

Turn left on Abbott and continue north to Gillon. You'll cross Euclid, an extra-wide street where the trolley turned and traveled on its way to its turnaround at Fairfield and Mockingbird. (Abbott Street is covered in the Abbott Walk.) Many early houses had speaking tubes in front. You'd pull the tube back and blow into it, and it would whistle. Whoever was inside would go to the other end and you could talk.

Turn left on Gillon. Prairie houses were often large and imposing structures, such as the early home at 3501 Gillon, built in 1913 (though it is an eclectic style and not typical). The dominant style for smaller houses until the early twenties was the Craftsman style, and one-story Craftsman "bungalows" were the rage. The house at 3505 Gillon, built around 1912, exemplifies how Craftsman style differs from the horizontal lines of the Prairie style. The low-pitched roof is usually gabled, often facing the front, with rafters frequently exposed from wide, unenclosed eave overhangs. Commonly seen are decorative beams or braces under the gables. Porches often have smaller front-facing gables, and the columns typically have a short, square or sloping upper section supported by a more massive pier that continues to ground level (though this porch has no massive supporting pier). Occasionally Tudor false half-timbering is used, such as you see here. The houses at 3518 and 3522 Gillon have more typical Craftsman-style columns.

Opposite. In the early 1900s gas heaters were replacing woodburning fireplaces and had become a status symbol. *Beau Monde* magazine carried several ads extolling the virtues of gas heat. *Courtesy of the Dallas Public Library*

The first home in Highland Park, built by Michael Costello in 1907, was moved to Old City Park in 1986. *Photo by Glenn Galloway*

Turn right on Byron and right again on Lindenwood to reach a veritable gold mine of Craftsman bungalows in the 3500 block of Lindenwood. There are plenty to choose from starting at 3517, with its unusual wood siding, and including 3512, 3510, 3509, 3508, 3507, 3505, and 3503.

Turn left on Auburndale and then right on Harvard. The real challenge comes in the 3400 block of Harvard, where you'll find both Prairie and Craftsman homes, sometimes with styles a bit mixed. Because the lots are smaller, the Prairie homes here were built on a smaller scale than others you've seen. You'll be able to spot a unique Craftsman style at 3410 right away because of the creek stones in the columns and the detailing on the gables. Among the homes to choose from are 3417, 3410, 3409, and 3408.

The grandest Craftsman home in the Park Cities was located on Lakeside Drive, surrounded by period homes. (See the Exall Lake Walk.) Much larger in scale than the bungalow homes you have just passed, it was a landmark example of a style whose characteristics would be echoed in the details of modern styles of the fifties and sixties. Unfortunately, it has been torn down.

Another day you may also enjoy walking along Maplewood and Stratford, south of Mockingbird, or in the 3800 block of Miramar, to view Prairie-style homes.

Swing left at Hillcrest and again at Dartmouth. With the demise of the Arts and Crafts Movement after World War I, one of the styles that supplanted the earlier popular forms was the Cape Cod home. The residence at 3402 Dartmouth is a landmark example, with its original cypress siding. This charming story-and-a-half house with the flagpole in front was designed by Flippen and Prather in 1919 and has received historic designation from the Park Cities Historical Society. The style was originally created to withstand severe New England winters. This home takes the fashionable gable-front form popular in the later Cape Cod designs. Notice the entry on the middle of the east side, with the original front door, and the oval plaque on the front of the home.

Having viewed an entire period of architectural development in the Park Cities, imagine what it must have been like to live in these early "modern" homes surrounded by rolling prairie, miles away from the nearest town. There must have been a village atmosphere.

You may choose to return to Armstrong by way of Abbott or Byron or any path you like, discovering your own favorite homes along the way. Wander among these streets filled with memories of horses tied up while friends visited, phonographs wound by hand to hear the music of Paderewski, cool evenings of conversation on wide porches watching the sun set, the trolley clanging as it carried people to see their first "moving picture" on Knox Street, Model T cars occasionally whizzing by, children on the lawns playing that new game, football—and, oh no! not a bath every night! This new plumbing is for the birds!

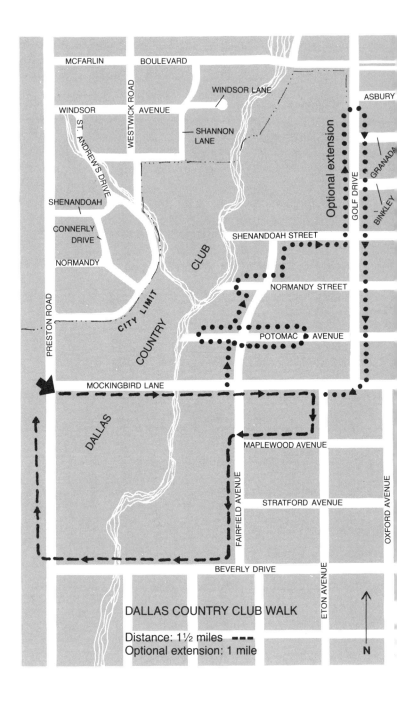

MCFARLIN   BOULEVARD

WINDSOR LANE

ASBURY

WINDSOR   AVENUE

WESTWICK ROAD

SHANNON LANE

ST. ANDREW'S DRIVE

Optional extension

GOLF DRIVE

GRANADA

BINKLEY

SHENANDOAH

SHENANDOAH STREET

CONNERLY DRIVE

NORMANDY

CLUB

CITY LIMIT

NORMANDY STREET

COUNTRY

POTOMAC   AVENUE

PRESTON ROAD

MOCKINGBIRD LANE

DALLAS

MAPLEWOOD AVENUE

FAIRFIELD AVENUE

STRATFORD AVENUE

OXFORD AVENUE

BEVERLY DRIVE

ETON AVENUE

DALLAS COUNTRY CLUB WALK

Distance: 1½ miles ▄▄▄
Optional extension: 1 mile

N

Dallas Country Club Walk

*Sometimes when I am sitting on the porch of the present
golf club, looking over the field, dreaming of the past and
looking to the future, I have thought I would like for the 6th
hole to be given my name. It's a short hole, where skill and
judgment, instead of brute strength, are required; surrounded with dimpling waters on two sides and the green
forest trees on two sides. I fancy that when I have crossed
over the Great Divide (if disembodied spirits are allowed to
visit the earth), it would be most pleasing to see my name
on the sand box at No. 6 and to hear, in answer to the
stranger's inquiry as to how that green came to have such
a name, the old golfer reply, "Why, that old chap was
the first president of the club, was president six or seven
years—and we liked him, hence the name."*
    *—J. T. Trezevant in "History of Dallas Country
        Club," 1913*

THUS IN HIS golden years J. T. Trezevant, first
president of the Dallas Country Club, waxed eloquent on a subject of particular importance to those
whose gait has slowed and whose hair has silvered to
soften the wrinkles that have begun to crease their
faces: What footprints will I leave on the sands of
time—or, in Trezevant's case, on the greens of the
country club?

Dallas Country Club Walk

WHEN J. T. Trezevant first swung a golf club in 1896, he knew he was hooked. He and some friends rented a room in Oak Lawn to keep their golf clubs and shoes in and rented thirty acres near what is now Lee Park so they could try their hand at the game together. The six greens were open prairie cleared of brush and weeds, with tin cans for holes and a barbed wire fence to keep the cattle out. By 1900 they had bought those thirty acres and incorporated under the name of "Dallas Golf and Country Club," which makes it the oldest country club in Texas and the second oldest in the United States. Trezevant became the first president. There were eight to ten original playing members, H. L. Edwards being the champion golfer then and for many years afterward.

Begin your walk at the corner of Preston Road and Mockingbird Lane and walk east on Mockingbird to view the 120-acre Dallas Country Club, which was relocated here in 1912. After you pass under the specially designed golf cart bridge, you can see to the north the new structure built in 1986 that houses four indoor tennis courts and two indoor racquetball courts. Also added at that time were the new brick fence, extensive additional landscaping, and renovations to the pool at a total cost of about $3 million. In contrast, early members were a frugal bunch, as the December 31, 1900, yearly income statement shows. Including fees for initiation, visitors, lockers, and golf balls, the income for the entire year came to $1,305.95. After expenditures were subtracted (taxes, labor, insurance), a total of $35.05 was left.

When Edgar Flippen and Hugh Prather began the development of their father-in-law's land in Highland Park, they faced a dilemma. Dallas was about four miles away and the roads were poor. How then would they lure the high class of residents they wished to attract to Highland Park and away from other developments? Dallas Golf and Country Club might be the answer! Flippen and Prather went to the owners of the Dallas Golf and Country Club and offered them 50 acres of the original 1,350 acres bought for Highland Park—at cost—if they would move their club. Adjoining property owners offered 65 acres at a slightly higher figure. In the final agreement, Dallas Golf and Country Club acquired 150 acres for about $30,000.

The acquisition of the club was a big coup, generating interest from well-heeled buyers in the property near the golf course that was being constructed. Although cotton was blooming on the yet uncleared acreage, 172 out of 186 lots were sold before the golf course was finished in 1912. Many believe Dallas Country Club was the biggest drawing card in bringing the very best element from Dallas and North Texas to exclusive Highland Park.

As you continue east you cross over Turtle Creek, which flows through the club. The bridge has been dubbed Mockingbird Lane Bridge and is dated 1923.

An optional side trip will take you north on Fairfield parallel to the path the creek takes through the golf course, which extends behind these homes all the way to McFarlin. This one-mile extension is purely a pleasure trip through a secluded neighborhood to give you a chance to enjoy the landscaping and homes that surround the country club greenbelt. **If you choose not to take this extension, simply read through the following three paragraphs and continue east along Mockingbird to Eton. To take the extension, turn left on Fairfield and walk a block north to Potomac.**

Just off Fairfield on Potomac are several homes designed by Anton Korn—3869 Potomac on the southeast corner, 3859 next door, and 3851 farther east; 3900 Potomac on the northwest corner; and 3921 farther west on the dead-end portion of Potomac. (See the Connor Lake Walk for more about Korn.) Two more modern homes by Enslie Oglesby of the Oglesby Group can be found on the dead-end portions of Potomac and Normandy, the next street to the north: 3929 Potomac, nestled among trees overlooking the creek, and 3918 Normandy, recently remodeled.

Continue north on Fairfield, turn right on Shenandoah, and left on Golf Drive. This will take you alongside the northern portion of the golf course, and into University Park. Legend has it that the Caddo Indians inhabited this area to hunt the buffalo which migrated here in the fall. They would kill the buffalo and make jerky for the winter. Although buffalo herds haven't roamed Highland Park since the 1880s, the wallows left by the herds can still be seen on the unplowed golf-course ground. According to Bill Crook, a longtime resident of the Park Cities, there are at least forty-eight or forty-nine wallows. **At a point near**

Opposite top. Dallas Golf and Country Club's first clubhouse, built in 1900 and located on Oak Lawn near what is now Lee Park, cost about $2,000 and contained a small locker room and clubroom. *Courtesy of Dallas Country Club*

Opposite. Saturday golfers are cooling off on the front steps of the golf shop of the Dallas Golf and Country Club located near Lemmon and Oak Lawn at Turtle Creek. *Courtesy of the First RepublicBank Park Cities*

Top. In 1904 the Dallas Golf and Country Club built a larger and more impressive clubhouse next to the first modest clubhouse on Oak Lawn. But in 1906 it burned just after the club hosted the first state golf tournament. *Courtesy of the Dallas Country Club*

Above. A third clubhouse for Dallas Golf and Country Club was erected in the then-popular Craftsman style on the same spot as the second, as shown in this 1909 photo. In the distance (located where Turtle Creek Village now stands) is Holy Trinity University, designed by H. A. Overbeck, which in 1910 was named Dallas University and later became Jesuit High School. *Courtesy of the Dallas Public Library*

the intersection of Golf and Asbury, peek through a break in the hedges to see the large indentations in the grass. These are most noticeable after a heavy rain when the water stands in the wallows. Keep a watchful eye out for poison ivy sneaking under the fence and onto your path.

Return south, staying on Golf Drive all the way back to Mockingbird. Turn right on Mockingbird to Eton Avenue. Mockingbird Lane got its name from the many mockingbirds found there, brashly mimicking other bird songs as they like to do. The white patches on the wings and tail of these gray birds make them relatively easy to identify. Long ago Mockingbird Lane was merely a trail which people followed to the creek to water their horses and mules.

Turn left on Eton and walk south to Maplewood, where a right turn brings you to a series of Colonial Revival homes. In the last ten years there has been an accelerated rate of change in residential structures in the Park Cities. Increased renovation has significantly altered many older homes, while many other houses have been demolished and replaced. Historical Revival predominates in the new homes, with Colonial Revival a favorite style. The facade is generally symmetrical with an accentuated center door. Those doors with a decorative crown (pediment) are of Georgian influence, while those with a fanlight above indicate Adam influence. The simple box-like style that almost entirely covers a typical Park Cities lot is commonly known as "Georgian." Nearly every street in the Park Cities has one.

On the northwest corner of Maplewood and Eton at 3800 Maplewood stands a Colonial Revival home built by Dr. and Mrs. R. W. Baird in 1913. The many columns distinguish it from its newer neighbors, and the fanlight over the door indicates Adam influence. The Bairds were prominent citizens of Highland Park in whose home was held the first meeting to discuss the organization of the Highland Park Methodist Church. There is a plaque in the church in their memory. In 1940 the home had a new owner, Wallace H. Savage, who would become mayor of Dallas in 1949. In 1980 the owner, George M. Underwood, III, requested Texas historic designation for the home.

In contrast to the Colonial Revival homes on the north side, across the street at 3819 Maplewood is an example of the more indigenous styles of architecture built when Highland Park was first developed. Representative of the Arts and Crafts Movement searching for a new American style, this is a Craftsman house. (For more information on this movement, see the Old Highland Park Walk.)

Continue west on Maplewood to Fairfield, cross to the country club side of the street, and turn south on Fairfield toward Beverly. If you will look closely at the street near the Dallas Country Club fence line, you can imagine the old trolley tracks running along there. Actually, they are still there, covered over when Fairfield was paved. The trolley came all the way from the Katy Railroad Station at Knox and Abbott. When the trolley reached the end of the line at Fairfield and Mockingbird, the conductor simply stopped and turned the seats to face the other direction since the trolley could not turn around. Then he headed back to the station. The ride cost five cents.

Plover hunting was once a great sport, probably as popular as dove hunting is today. Ted Dealey, editor of the *Dallas Morning News*, recalled slaying them by the scores in

3800 Maplewood

When the Dallas Golf and Country Club moved to Highland Park in 1912, this Tudor clubhouse was built on Turtle Creek. The

this area. Duck and rabbit hunting were popular, too. There were no big lakes in North Texas then and ducks by the thousands followed the Trinity River and its tributaries. Besides large quantities of migrating ducks, abundant plover, rabbits, and native mockingbirds, there were ground squirrels that burrowed in the prairie grass on what is now the golf course.

Turn right on Beverly Drive and continue west toward Preston. Beverly Drive is one of the most prestigious streets in the Park Cities, sought after for that reason alone, as well as for its spacious lots facing the wide street. Hugh Prather, Sr., and his wife, Johnetta Armstrong Prather, lived in several houses on Beverly. Among these was 4001 Beverly, at the corner of Highland Drive, where their daughter Anne Elizabeth was born. For a short time during the Depression they lived at 4015 Beverly.

roped-off area in the foreground is the swimming pool. *Courtesy of Dallas Public Library*

Edgar L. Flippen and his wife, Minnie May Armstrong Flippen, moved from their Mount Vernon–style estate at 4800 Preston in 1921 to 4025 Beverly, where they could enjoy a view of the greens of the Dallas Country Club as well as Exall Lake. The numerous hats Flippen wore must have made it difficult for him to get out the door in the morning—on the pile were his hats as president of the Flippen-Prather Realty Company, president of the First National Bank, and third president of the Dallas Country Club (which had moved across the street in 1912).

You may wonder what happened to the old Dallas Golf and Country Club in Oak Lawn. The old grounds, which had originally cost around $5,000, were sold at auction in 1912 for $122,000 cash. The new club in Highland Park was completed the same year and simply called Dallas Country Club. The new clubhouse overlooking the lake, a Prairie-style mansion, was built with a rambling Tudor influence, and faced Beverly Drive. Edgar Flippen became the new president. Membership was to be limited to five hundred, and qualifications were "integrity in business coupled with moral probity," together with the desire to participate in the "ancient and royal" game of golf.

In 1957 construction of a fashionable new 50,000-square-foot clubhouse facing Mockingbird, designed by Harper and Kemp, was completed with a price tag of $1,500,000. It included a 40-by-100-foot swimming pool, still in use today. The grand old Tudor clubhouse was torn down and grass was sodded to make a practice area for golfers.

Approaching Turtle Creek, use your imagination to envision the first Dallas Country Club swimming pool here. It was at the base of the limestone cliffs on the north side of Beverly, and to use the swimming hole, members had to climb down the cliffs, near where the spillway was later built. Daniel Otstott remembers swimming here as a boy, retrieving from the bottom golf balls which he and his enterprising friends then repainted and sold.

To the left of the creek was the Tudor clubhouse. To the right of the creek there were tables that were used for barbecues, and a swinging bridge that crossed the creek to reach them. Jesse Thomas, a bartender, remembers having to cross the bridge to serve those tables. He recalls that the bridge would start swinging and the plates of food would slide right off the trays into the creek. Sometimes the cook couldn't understand why waiters returned so quickly for more plates.

On the southeast corner of Beverly and Preston is the estate of wealthy oilman Ed Cox, formerly the Rose Lloyd mansion. The relationship between socialite Rose Lloyd and the Dallas Country Club was not always a smooth one, as you'll see in the Pecan Tree Walk.

Step inside the gateway of the country club for a final view of the grounds. To return to your starting point, cross Preston and turn north. And savor one last tidbit of information. A new member accepted into Dallas Country Club in 1912 could join by buying two hundred dollars worth of stock.

A group of golfers are shown gathered on the first tee of the newly built Dallas Country Club in 1912. *Photo by Frank Rogers and Son, courtesy of the First RepublicBank Park Cities*

A 1925 photo shows Preston Road looking south near the intersection of Edmondson. On the left are the greens of the Dallas Country Club. *Courtesy of the Dallas Public Library*

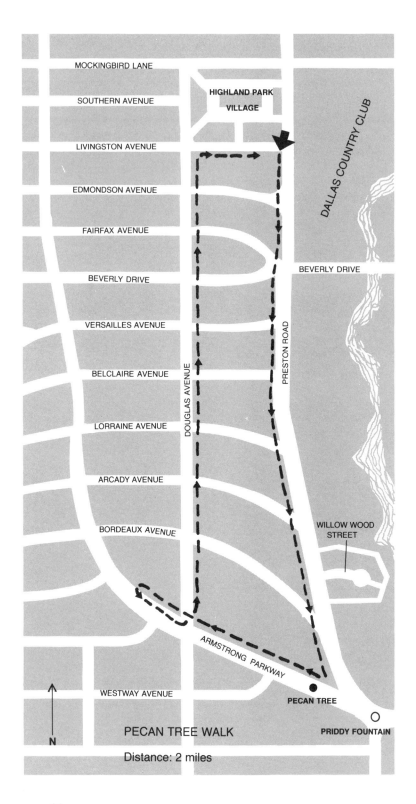

MOCKINGBIRD LANE

SOUTHERN AVENUE

HIGHLAND PARK VILLAGE

LIVINGSTON AVENUE

EDMONDSON AVENUE

FAIRFAX AVENUE

BEVERLY DRIVE

BEVERLY DRIVE

VERSAILLES AVENUE

BELCLAIRE AVENUE

LORRAINE AVENUE

ARCADY AVENUE

BORDEAUX AVENUE

WILLOW WOOD STREET

DALLAS COUNTRY CLUB

DOUGLAS AVENUE

PRESTON ROAD

ARMSTRONG PARKWAY

WESTWAY AVENUE

PECAN TREE

PECAN TREE WALK

PRIDDY FOUNTAIN

Distance: 2 miles

N

Pecan Tree Walk

THIS IS A walk for all seasons, sparkling with holiday decorations and lights at Christmas, a must on anyone's "let's go look at the lights" list—and resplendent with nature's own glories in the spring. It features what has been called "the world's greatest Christmas Tree," the Pecan Tree on Armstrong, designated by the Park Cities Historical Society in December, 1986, as a historic landmark, with a plaque to prove it! This site, perhaps above all others, represents the heart of Highland Park.

The many lovely estates along Beverly and Armstrong bespeak the genteel life of immaculate lawns and spacious mansions. But it's the thriving pecan tree, over 120 years old, that people come from miles around to see. The tree and the land were once owned by the family of Highland Park's first resident and physician, Dr. John Cole. When he claimed the land in 1843, Cole used this area for planting. His son Joe continued on the farm after Dr. Cole's death.

In the spring of 1865, Joe returned from the Civil War wearing a tattered uniform and riding an old mule. A Negro field hand working for the Coles claimed he looked like a scarecrow dressed in rags. Just twenty-three years old, Joe had had three horses shot from under him and was sick and tired of the killing and destruction he'd seen in the war. A few weeks later when Joe was plowing the fields, he accidentally uprooted a small pecan sapling. So surprised was he to see a young tree in the middle of the field, Joe jumped down from his wagon and replanted it, asking the field hand to brace it with a nearby fence post. Joe gave strict orders that the tree be allowed to grow. His family nurtured it and watched it grow, adding a deed restriction, when the land was later sold, that the tree should remain.

Town fathers simply built a parkway for the tree, and it continues to stand today, decorated with lights in a special ceremony each Christmas season. It stands sixty-five feet high and over sixty feet wide. It takes four men four days to install the more than twelve hundred lights. Since 1927 only in two instances have the lights not shone at Christmastime: during the four years of World War II and during the 1973 energy crisis.

This 1923 aerial photo shows Highland Park West newly laid out with the pecan tree in its parkway and sapling trees lining the first streets. On the left is the lake now called Connor Lake, and on the right below Preston Road is Exall Lake. *Courtesy of the Dallas Public Library*

Pecan Tree Walk

BEGIN your walk just south of Highland Park Village and walk south on Preston Road. You'll see the grounds of the Dallas Country Club on your left, across Preston. The club has come a long way since its origins on Oak Lawn when a six-hole golf course on the prairie included tin cans for holes and barbed wire to keep the cattle out, and its members sent away to Wright and Ditson in Boston for their golf balls. (See the Dallas Country Club Walk.)

The area east of Turtle Creek and Preston Road is Old Highland Park, begun in 1907. The area on your right is Highland Park West and was opened in 1924. From the outset the master plans called for plenty of parks, and developers donated sufficient right-of-way for an extra-wide thoroughfare for Preston Road, the first paved road in Highland Park. A planted parkway leads all the way to Armstrong.

Listening to the roar of the traffic whizzing by, try to imagine the problems caused by traffic on unpaved roads. The dust problem from dirt roads in the early days of Dallas caused Highland Park to advertise itself as "beyond the city's dust and smoke"—undoubtedly a strong selling point for people weary of battling the constant dust that filtered into their homes.

Over a hundred years ago vast herds of Longhorn steers were driven up what is now Preston Road to the Chisholm Trail to Kansas markets and railheads. Preston Road follows the same trail that John Neely Bryan followed when he built his cabin on the Trinity where Dallas began. The trail was named for William G. Preston, a Republic of Texas army captain stationed at a fort on a curve in the Red River near a good landing place. When he left the army, Preston installed a ferry at what became known as Preston's Bend. Today Preston Road as well as many businesses, shopping centers, churches, and other institutions bear his name.

The tree-shaded portion of Preston between Beverly and Armstrong, so stunning in the spring when the azaleas bloom, was known as Bridle Path Park in the 1920s. Many women in the neighborhood owned horses or rented them from Heady's Stables west of the old Cotton Belt Railroad (now the Dallas North Tollway) for a ride down Bridle Path

Park. While the ladies were posting along sidesaddle in their formal riding clothes, young men would ride flat out across the prairie in pursuit of jackrabbits.

As you walk this portion, take note of some of the magnificent estates that have filled this prairie, and the history behind them. One of the most colorful ladies of the day, Rose Lloyd, lived in the huge mansion at the southeast corner of Preston and Beverly. The daughter of a wealthy banker–plantation owner from Shreveport, Mrs. A. T. Lloyd opened her home for lavish parties and club meetings. Once when her garden club met on the terrace of her home overlooking Turtle Creek, Mrs. Lloyd noticed an odor coming from the creek. Mortified, she learned that the Dallas Country Club across the road was running its sewage lines into the creek. After paying a builder $5,000 to cement the drain shut overnight, Mrs. Lloyd called the club's manager. "It will be to your advantage to be sure the men do not run the showers in the locker room," she informed him. The country club had to build a brand-new sewage system. Some years later when the club offered to buy her property, Mrs. Lloyd, indignant, offered to buy the Dallas Country Club!

Another house with a fascinating history is the home of Governor William Clements in the next block at 4800 Preston Road. Originally built in 1910 by Edgar Flippen, it was to serve as his home as well as part of the promotion of Highland Park. The house has been remodeled several times since being designed and constructed by C. D. Hill as a replica of Mount Vernon. Before Bill Clements bought the mansion it had belonged to A. Pollard Simons. When Simons died in 1975, the property was willed to the Town of Highland Park, with specific instructions that it be used as a youth center, library, or art museum, with $12,000 per year set aside for upkeep. If the estate was not so used, the title was to pass to Southern Methodist University. The town finally reached an agreement whereby the property could be sold, with half of the proceeds from the sale going to Simons's widow, the other half to Highland Park and SMU. In 1977 SMU received two-thirds of fifty percent of the sale and Highland Park received one-third of fifty percent. The Highland Park share of the money, which amounted to about $165,000, was put into a fund for the upkeep of its parks.

The Colonial Revival home at 4700 Preston was originally built by Hugh Prather, Sr., in 1917 and is now the John Black estate. The architect was Anton Korn.

For those of us who have grown up with electricity, plumbing, and other amenities, it is humbling to realize that our pioneer forefathers often arrived with little more than a dream. Through their perseverance and hard work they forged the way of life that Park Cities residents now enjoy.

One of the most important pioneers in the history of Highland Park was its first resident, Dr. John Cole. He arrived in 1843 (not long after John Neely Bryan established the settlement that would become Dallas) bringing with him his wife, Polly, their nine children, and specimens of fruit trees. The Republic of Texas gave Cole a land grant of 640 acres as a member of the Peters Colony, the company that brought early settlers to Texas. Eventually Cole owned all the land from Abbott to Lomo Alto and Mockingbird to Blackburn. Not only was Cole the first resident of Highland Park, he was also its first physician and pharmacist and even became the first probate judge of Dallas County. Most of the land that is Highland Park today originally belonged to the Cole family.

At what is now 4500 Preston, Dr. Cole built his first log house on the lot where real estate magnate Trammell Crow now resides, formerly the H. L. Edwards mansion. Cole's orchard filled with peaches, grapes, and herbs from which he made medicines was located where the B. D. Saxon home is today at 4400 Preston, on the corner of Preston and Armstrong.

As you approach the intersection of Preston and Armstrong, note the fountain on the island in the middle of Preston, dedicated to the memory of Ashley Priddy, former Highland Park mayor (1970–1975).

Turn west on Armstrong Parkway. Cole Park and Cole Avenue bear John Cole's name, but perhaps the greatest tribute to his pioneer spirit is the pecan tree you see here in the parkway, over 120 years old, planted by his son Joe. **Walk over to the parkway to see the historic marker placed there in 1986.** Joseph Larkin Cole was only eighteen months old when his family arrived in this area, and as a boy he killed quail, ducks, squirrels, and deer on this land. Dr. Cole died in 1851 when little Joe was only nine, but Joe continued to help farm what is now Highland Park West, and helped run stock and Morgan horses in the area east of

This photo of the famous pecan tree was taken from Preston Road looking west in 1910 before Armstrong Parkway was paved. *Courtesy of the First RepublicBank Park Cities*

Turtle Creek. At nineteen Joe mounted a Morgan horse and proudly rode off to join the Civil War.

It was Joe who, in the spring of 1865, returned riding an old mule instead of his fine horse, a few weeks later planting the magnificent tree you see before you. At twenty-three, he'd seen enough of death and wanted to experience life. By the time Joe had children, the tree had grown enough that his first-born daughter, Mary, could have her first playhouse under the shade of its branches. Joe lived here until 1888, when he sold the land for $120 an acre, stipulating that the pecan tree should not be disturbed. It has become a Highland Park legend.

When Highland Park West was being laid out, George Kessler, who had drawn plans for the city of Dallas in 1911, was hired to develop a master plan. Determined to preserve the pecan tree, then fifty years old, developers Edgar Flippen and Hugh Prather thought about replanting it. As lots were being plotted, offers for the lot with the tree went as high, according to rumor, as a million dollars. The developers decided to lay out the street in such a way that the tree would have its own parkway. The Cole family burial plot was located within the shadow of the tree, and these graves were moved to Greenwood Cemetery. Highland Park West was opened in 1924 as "Country Club Estates,

When Highland Park West opened in 1924, the "Million Dollar Pecan Tree" stood in its own parkway, serving as the entry point to Armstrong Parkway. *Courtesy of the First RepublicBank Park Cities*

the Pasadena of the South," with the pecan tree as the entry point to Armstrong Parkway.

Realizing what a drawing card this "Million Dollar Pecan Tree" was, the Prather family began in 1927 to decorate it for Christmas, a tradition that marks the start of the season for many families who turn out to sing carols and witness the lighting of the big tree. This is a beautiful area to walk at Christmas with children, and a must to drive by during Christmas at night. In 1951 another pecan tree was planted nearby "just in case" because some of the branches on the old tree were cracking. The second tree is actually descended from the first, for it was grown from one of its pecans.

The pecan tree may be the main attraction but there are also many stately and beautiful homes in this district, built in a variety of architectural styles. **On the northwest corner of Preston and Armstrong,** at 4401 Preston, is a Spanish Eclectic home, one of the few Spanish homes that is big enough to have its own interior courtyard. **Begin walking west on Armstrong.** On the south side of the parkway are several different styles in a row: a Neoclassical at 4211, a Tudor at 4217, and a formal Spanish Eclectic with unusual detailing, designed by Fooshee and Cheek, at 4225. The distinctive red brick house at 4224 Armstrong, designed by

Hal Thomson, has a twin on Swiss Avenue. Directly across the parkway at 4237 is a wonderful Tudor house built in stone with brick detailing around the windows. This is unusual, as most Tudor houses are built in brick with stone detailing around the windows. The very formal and symmetrical gray house at 4236 with the flared roofline and round-topped dormers is a beautiful French Renaissance designed by Hal Thomson, who also designed the house at 4242. A stately French house can be found at 4248, with its two end wings, called twin pavilions.

Continue west on Armstrong across Douglas. The house at 4320 Armstrong has been designated a historic landmark, chosen for its architectural significance, by the Park Cities Historical Society. The plaque is inside the simple arched opening leading to the front door. The house was designed by J. J. Patterson in 1938 in the French Eclectic style, with a prominent round tower, and is now owned by Leslie Lippitt Clark. Notice the variety of different exterior materials—brick, stone, concrete, stucco, and wood.

Return to Douglas, turn left, and walk north on Douglas. You'll pass a beautiful greenbelt area between Armstrong and Bordeaux called Douglas Park, comprising nearly two acres. (You may wish to return to view some of the homes on Bordeaux in the Versailles Walk.)

Continue north on Douglas to return to Highland Park Village. As you walk this portion, enjoy the many homes of varied styles that catch your eye. The Colonial Revival home on the northeast corner of Lorraine and Douglas at 4236 Lorraine might not immediately attract your attention. It resembles a seventeenth century Salem house. Notice the overhang with drops underneath. And don't miss the Tudor home with three chimney pots on the northwest corner of Belclaire and Douglas at 4300 Belclaire.

High property values here are due not only to the extensive greenbelt land which you see, but also to Highland Park's strict property deed restrictions. Blueprints of the homes you are passing in Highland Park West had to be submitted to an architectural committee for approval. Highland Park still will not issue a building permit without this stipulation. In addition, retail business in Highland Park is largely restricted to the Highland Park Village area and the outer edges of the community, rather than being scattered throughout. Deed and zoning restrictions, coupled with the excellent school system, insure that the value of homes in this area will continue to be high.

Unlike Dallas, Houston, and other sprawling cities of the twentieth century with development widely scattered along freeways, far from police and fire protection and often with inadequate sewer and water connections, Highland Park was developed in a more people-oriented fashion. It was built in a limited area close to its city services, around abundant parkways and beautiful creeks, with many trees planted and sidewalks placed for the enjoyment of its residents, and with its retail development largely confined to one area.

Turn right on Livingston just south of the Village to return to Preston. As you conclude your walk, ponder how different this community might have been with several developers with conflicting ideas instead of one set of developers with a coordinated plan and a single vision. The old pecan tree is a symbol that dreams do indeed become realities, that even in the face of war and destruction life goes on.

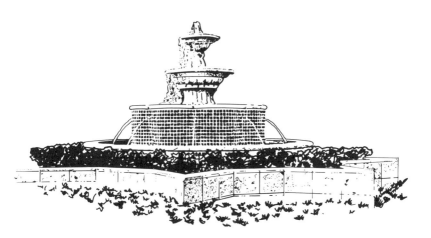

Highland Park Village Walk

WHEN "Miss Willie" Sterett ran the S&S Tearoom in Highland Park Village, if she thought people were staying too long she'd pick up the microphone, call their names, and ask, "Would you please leave?"

A no-nonsense business woman with a husky voice, "Miss Willie," as everyone called her, and her sister Mrs. Margaret Staten brought the Tearoom to the Village in 1931. The daughters of Dallas pioneer W. L. Sterett, the sisters had begun the business in their home on Knox Street, using one card table and dishes bought at the ten-cent store.

From the time the Tearoom opened in the Village, it became an "in" place for ladies to meet and enjoy good food and company in a genteel atmosphere. As time passed, even a few men discovered the delights of the S&S Tearoom, a Highland Park landmark for nearly sixty years.

Under new ownership after 1957, the Tearoom was one of the last bastions of another era, still popular and still crowded at lunchtime, mostly with well-dressed longtime patrons in their sixties and seventies. Its lease expired in October of 1987, and its owner conceded that the high rent would now force the S&S Tearoom to abandon its landmark status and move to another location, at Inwood Village on Lovers Lane.

Whatever the fate of this lunchtime institution, the ghosts of Miss Willie and her following will continue to be a part of the aura of Highland Park Village. Alas for whatever business moves in to replace it—the

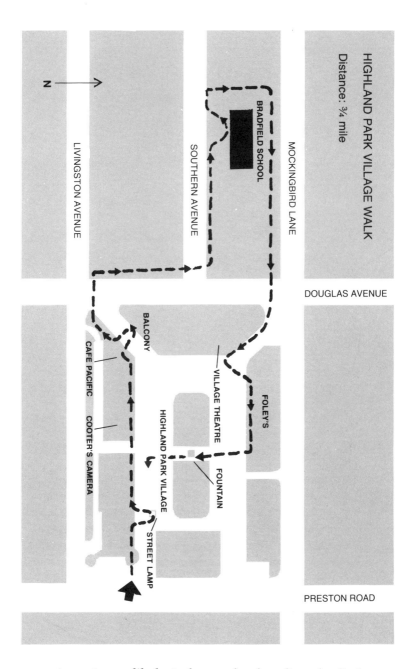

N →

LIVINGSTON AVENUE

SOUTHERN AVENUE

BRADFIELD SCHOOL

MOCKINGBIRD LANE

DOUGLAS AVENUE

BALCONY

CAFE PACIFIC

COOTER'S CAMERA

VILLAGE THEATRE

HIGHLAND PARK VILLAGE

FOLEY'S

FOUNTAIN

STREET LAMP

PRESTON ROAD

new tenants are likely to hear a husky, disembodied voice intoning, "So and so . . . would you please leave?"

Highland Park Village Walk

THE HIGHLAND Park Village is the prototype for shopping centers all over the country. Built in 1931, it was the first planned shopping center in the United States with a unified architectural style and stores facing in toward an interior parking area, all built and managed under single ownership. Kansas City's Country Club Plaza was built earlier, in 1920, but the stores faced the street and did not provide on-site parking. Highland Park Village is the only unified retail development in all of Highland Park's 2.2 square miles.

This trend-setting shopping center was built by the same developers who had opened Highland Park in 1907 and Highland Park West in 1924, Hugh Prather, Sr., and Edgar Flippen. They decided Highland Park needed a shopping center that could also function as a town square. With the same foresight they had shown in their earlier ventures, they gave the project much thought and careful planning. They were courageous to attempt it, because most bankers and merchants offered discouraging words, stating that business was "expected" to stay downtown. Before the eventual design was chosen, the developers traveled to Barcelona, Spain, as well as to California and Mexico, to study the architecture. The style finally chosen was Mediterranean Spanish. Marion Fooshee and James Cheek were chosen as the architects. Notice the tile roofs with little overhang, arches above doors and windows, overhanging balconies, wrought iron embellishments by Potter Iron Works, ornate tilework, and brick paths and walkways.

Begin your walk on Preston at the corner of the row of shops on the south side of the Village, and walk west into the shopping center. By 1931, homes were already built all around the Village except to the east where the well-manicured golfing greens of the Dallas Country Club were easily visible through the row of small trees that lined their land. The streets and spaces for the Village were already laid out the way you see them today, except there was not a single tree, and only a few buildings.

Walk out into the central parking area to the first street lamp you see. Fortunately the old lamps have been retained and not "modernized." In the concrete in which the

When Highland Park Village opened in 1931 the only buildings were a gas station on Preston, a sales office in the middle section, and the first retail section in the southwest part of the Village. Highland Park West and Loma Linda had just opened, as evidenced by the small trees planted west, north, and south of the Village. There are golfers on the green of the first hole at the Dallas Country Club. *Courtesy of the First RepublicBank Park Cities*

lamp is anchored notice the inscription, Central Bitulithic Company, 1930. Two other lamps in the Village bear this inscription.

Continue west to where Cooter's Camera is today. Notice the oval Park Cities Historical Society plaque on the east side of the doorway, and the bronze plaque commemorating the Golden Anniversary of the Village on the west side. (The building fronting on Preston in the center section of the Village has been excluded from the Park Cities historic designation, for architectural reasons.) When the Village opened in 1931, the only retail section was this one where Cooter's is presently located. The grand opening of the Village in 1931, according to a longtime resident, was a thrilling event. There were booths in the center sec-

In the thirties the A&P grocery was among the stores located in the first retail section of the Highland Park Village. *Courtesy of the Park Cities Historical Society*

tion, and a Ferris wheel—it was a real party. Nearly everyone in town came, and the Village was off to a great start.

This first retail building contained two grocery stores. The A&P was here for all the ladies to buy their basic groceries, but for high-style shopping you could have a clerk pick out your "gourmet" grocery items at Hunt's. If you didn't want to cook you could eat at the S&S Tearoom, also located in this section. Later it moved to a spot on the west side, in the same section as the Village Theatre.

The tenant that remained in the Village the longest (from 1931 until 1987) was the S&S Tearoom, a stately restaurant with a colorful background. Those who have lived in Dallas a long time remember hearing of Col. Bill Sterett, a vigorous individual with a daughter who, though married twice, was known as "Miss Willie." She and her sister Margaret had a restaurant on Knox Street whose reputation was bigger than their small establishment. In order to entice them to move to the Village, Hugh Prather gave them three months free rent.

Their S&S Tearoom flourished and became one of the institutions of the town. But very few men frequented the establishment, and for a very good reason. If asked, Miss Willie would tell you that she didn't like men because they ate too much! In fact, in the Sterett tradition she had an answer for most anything one asked. When someone inquired about their delicious coffee, she announced that she bought it over at the A&P, the cheapest brand she could find, and then boiled the hell out of it. Their "tearoom" actually served only one kind of tea; mostly they served coffee. Miss Willie probably named it a tearoom to keep the men out. Besides, how could it cater to men? It had no men's room! After twenty-six successful years, even without encouraging male customers, the Steretts sold their business in 1957 to Mildred Libberton. It was then managed and later owned by her niece, Barbara Fisher.

From Cooter's Camera, continue west past Cafe Pacific, which has a peaceful patio and flowing fountain around the corner. Directly across from Cafe Pacific is a balcony with hand-painted as well as hand-hewn ceiling beams. Fine handwork such as this is becoming a rarity.

Cross Douglas and head north, then turn left on Southern for a side trip around Bradfield School. Along the way, notice that the Spanish decor of the Village has been maintained on all sides.

The school land extends from Douglas to Armstrong and was purchased in 1924 for $16,000. Highland Park West and the Loma Linda development had just opened, and new children were being added to the district rapidly as new houses sprang up. Armstrong School, the only elementary school at that time, was bursting its seams. A new high school (now the middle school) was built in 1922, which helped relieve the situation somewhat. But a bond issue was passed in 1925 for $250,000 to build not only this new elementary school, which opened in 1926, but also University Park School in 1928 for the population rapidly spreading north in University Park. Each cost approximately $125,000 and each was built by Rogers & O'Rourke using the same set of plans designed by architects Otto H. Lang and Frank Witchell. Both new schools received teachers as well as pupils from Armstrong School, which can be called their alma mater.

The school you see in front of you was named for John Sherman Bradfield, not only in honor of his length of service as president of the school board (1917–1933), but also for his wisdom and devotion to schools and to his community. **Walk up to the school to get a closer look at the ornate pediment over the front door, with its decorative shields.** Above the pediment the date is clearly marked, 1926. The tile roof with little overhang ties the building in with the Spanish architecture of the Village. Take note of the plain

The Village Theatre (shown under construction) opened in 1935, the first luxury suburban theater in Texas. In the distance is Bradfield School. *Courtesy of Pat's Park Cities Delicatessen*

beige brickwork. The east wing was obviously added later, because its brick does not match and its doorway has no decoration. The west wing has an ornate pediment.

Turn right at the west corner of the school and walk around the end of the building toward Mockingbird. As you circle the building, study the color of the bricks to see where new sections were added. On the northeast corner it's evident where the old and new bricks were blended together.

Turn right at Mockingbird and walk past the playground back toward the Village. Cross Douglas with the light and walk back into the Village toward the theater, passing another flowing fountain. In 1935 with great fanfare the Village Theatre opened, the first luxury suburban theater in Texas. Built at a cost of $100,000 with a seating capacity for 1,350, it has been a popular entertainment spot ever since. Next door was Martha Washington's Ice Cream Parlor, a favorite of movie-goers. Until the theater was

A letter mailed from the Village Post Office, located in what was then the Sanger Harris building, would be postmarked "Village, Texas." *Courtesy of Hugh Prather, Jr.*

leased in 1987 to American-Multi-Cinema, the second largest theater chain in the United States, it claimed to be the last independently run theater in the nation's ten largest cities to show first-run films. The new owners redesigned it into four auditoriums, preserving the art deco style of the original.

The year 1935 was a busy one, for besides the theater, Safeway (now Tom Thumb) also opened, as well as Volk Brothers. At that time Volk's just sold shoes, only later becoming a department store, and everyone thought Mr. Volk was crazy to be the first owner of a downtown store to open a suburban outlet. But in just a few years the store doubled in size and it seemed that everyone in the Park Cities was wearing Volk shoes.

Cross to the north row of shops and walk east toward Preston. You'll pass Foley's, formerly Sanger-Harris, which joined Volk Brothers in 1941. At that time it was simply called Sanger's. Inside were not only fashionable clothes but also a post office. The ornate facade of these buildings shows Moorish influence. By this time nearly all the buildings you see around you had sprung up, and the only parts of the Village that were not complete were this north row of buildings and the building in the center section that fronts on Preston.

World War II prevented other stores from following right away into the Village, but after the war and the ensuing postwar baby boom came the retail exodus to the suburbs. Another grand opening in 1951 was memorable for the traffic jams it caused up and down Preston and Mockingbird. Doak Walker was a local football hero at Highland Park High School who had become a national sports figure when he won the Heisman Trophy as a player for Southern Methodist University. He went on to play with the Detroit Lions. Doak Walker's Sporting Goods store opened in 1951 with a throng of admirers lining up for autographs from Doak and two other football heroes, Bobby Layne and Kyle Rote. Once a popular gathering spot for young people, Doak Walker's store soon outgrew its location here and moved to Inwood Village.

Many stores have come and gone. In 1966 the Howard Corporation bought the Village and it began to go downhill. In 1976 real estate magnate Henry S. Miller bought it from them for $5 million and has taken a personal interest in restoring the facades, planning additional landscaping and plantings, and upgrading the stores. It has meant that some old standbys like Hall's Variety and Oshman's are no longer here. But in their place are chic new boutiques and trendy restaurants. With the upgrading of stores and restaurants, the fate of the only remaining original tenant, the S&S Tearoom, was sealed when they were unable to renew their lease in 1987.

In 1981 the Village's Golden Anniversary was celebrated with a grand party called "Fiesta 50." An annual Christmas celebration features an appearance by Santa Claus. Several miles of lights and several huge Christmas trees adorn the Village each Christmastime.

Don't miss a stroll through the center section with its central fountain. And before you leave the Village, take time to browse in some of the interesting shops that give the center its exclusiveness as well as its charm. This popular showplace has a variety of stores to offer. With its many trees, benches throughout its neatly landscaped areas, and even discreetly placed bike racks, you know you're in a special place.

Notice how the original design of the Village provided for loading zones in back of the stores for food and merchandise so that trucks would not have to be on the plaza during business hours. As you wander around, keep an eye out for the architectural detail that has made the Village an architectural landmark. Compare it with other shopping centers and you'll begin to see why this ten-acre prototype development, carved out of Texas prairie land, has been called the most beautiful shopping center in the Southwest.

Versailles Walk

THE JOYS of walking are myriad. We can smell the flowers, learn about trees, watch the cloud formations change as a front approaches, hear the insects and birds, observe the landscape change with the seasons, and see the textures and colors of our world around us. And while we're having a good time, walking is also a good way to get rid of fatigue, stress, boredom, anger, or sluggishness.

The Walkways Center in Washington, D.C., estimates that more than fifty-five million people are walking for exercise and fitness. That's about one-fourth of all the people in the United States. Walking burns calories, improves muscle tone, and increases blood flow. This in turn increases cardiovascular fitness. As heart muscles strengthen, the heart pumps less and can rest more between beats. Improved circulation helps cells use oxygen more efficiently. You can think more clearly. And your blood pressure may even drop as you walk away tension and anxiety caused by "stress."

Dr. Hans Selye, founder of the International Institute of Stress, gained fame for his pioneering medical studies which showed how prolonged physical and mental stress can help cause many common degenerative diseases such as heart attacks, high blood pressure, ulcers, and even cancer. Author of over thirty books, Selye states that stress is reflected in the rate of wear and tear on the body. The human body, like tires on a car, wears longest when it wears evenly.

Walkers can relieve their stress-related anxieties and ease their overworked minds with the soothing rhythm of a relaxed stride and a breath of fresh air.

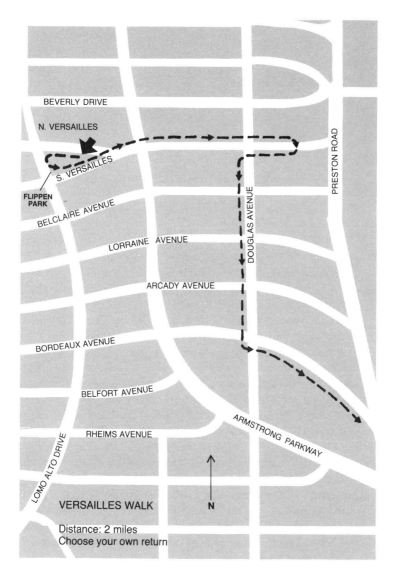

The effect is to smooth out tensions and bring our bodies and minds back into balance with nature, letting the storms of our lives blow themselves out. How many times have you returned from a walk wondering why you were so upset earlier, or with a solution to a problem that had been bothering you? For its sheer beauty, the Versailles Walk is a good one for walking your cares away, so that you can return ready to meet the day's challenges, or even its petty routines, with new resolve.

Versailles Walk

Once more a perfect morn! With feet that trod
Earth's green and sun-kissed hair that's swept heaven's
blue
Affable, smiling and aweless—I met God,
Delighted with His work as when it was new.
          —Sir William Watson, "Epigram on Morn"

FIND YOURSELF a perfect morn—perhaps one in early spring—and make the Versailles Walk a day-starter. It's a fairly long walk, but an invigorating one, especially in the cool of an April or May morning when the dew still washes over the grass and spring flowers are at their most glorious.

Begin your walk in Flippen Park, at Versailles and Lomo Alto, where you may find azaleas and daffodils in bloom. Officially designated as Flippen Park in 1930, it has been dubbed Echo Park by the neighbors because the gazebo at its center echoes. The striking pavilion was designed by architects Fooshee and Cheek and built in 1929 by Edgar Flippen and Hugh Prather. Like the Loma Linda walls you'll see on the Loma Linda Walk, the gazebo was built in the Spanish Colonial Revival style. Painted wrought iron lacework circles through the arches of the octagonal structure, which looks almost like a fancy wedding cake placed in the middle of a miniature garden. The stucco walls feature scrolls encircling the arches, leading to a red tile hipped roof. It is the softly curved ceiling that creates the echo. The floor is made of multicolored slate pieces set in concrete and trimmed in red brick.

East of the gazebo you'll see an elegant fountain in what was once a simple reflecting pool. In the late sixties, Lambert's Landscape planted the azalea beds that adorn the pool and gazebo. The fountain is a relatively new addition to the park, dedicated in 1976 to Ruby Lee McElroy, who lived nearby on Westway. The McElroy family and various friends and neighbors contributed to the purchase of the fountain and gave it to the Town of Highland Park. The original fountain, ordered from Italy of native Italian stone, was destroyed by vandals and a replacement had to be installed. At the west end of the pool, you will see a bronze dedication marker. Several benches throughout the

park invite the visitor to stop and rest and drink in the natural and manmade beauty of the area. In 1987 the park received historic designation from the Park Cities Historical Society, with the oval plaque located on the north side of the gazebo.

As you circle the park, following the sidewalk under numerous cedar and other trees, note the many Colonial Revival homes that surround it. Homes in this style generally have a two-story symmetrical facade with an accentuated front door.

Begin walking east along Versailles, toward Douglas. You'll pass one of the sturdiest live oak trees in the Park Cities at the corner of Armstrong. Notice the pink home with the black and white trim at 4324 Versailles. This Spanish Renaissance home is unusual for its style because it is symmetrical. **Continue across Douglas** to see 4221 Versailles, an Italian Renaissance home with its arches and wide roof overhang. **Then turn back to Douglas and swing south about five blocks, until you reach Bordeaux.**

Highland Park West, as this development was originally called, was an expansion of Highland Park in the mid-1920s. Although the topography was considered rather uninspiring, the developer varied the lot sizes to fit the gracefully curving streets, and added greenbelts and parks to give each street an identity of its own. Today many old trees and a profusion of flowering color lend a serene beauty to these peaceful streets. As you walk, listen to the songs of the birds chirping in the branches of the trees. You may see gardeners arriving at the various homes to do their handiwork. It's easy to imagine the milkman and the iceman of an earlier day joining the procession as they made their morning rounds.

Turn left and walk east on Bordeaux. Note the mysterious, almost foreboding Italian Renaissance home next to the landscaped lot on the southeast corner of Douglas and Bordeaux. The home at 4271 Bordeaux, with its natural stone facade, is a wonderful example of the Italian Renaissance style. Italian Renaissance homes were almost always done either in stone or yellow brick or stucco. Red brick was reserved for English Renaissance homes (Georgian and Colonial). Designed by architect Hal Thomson and built in 1928, this home is typical of the period. It is symmetrical with a tall roof and wide overhanging eaves, and the windows on the second story are smaller than those on the ground floor. An arched entryway completes the authenticity of this period home. Thomson, who moved to Dallas from Austin in 1907, built many of the homes on this block. During later years his partner was Frank Swain.

Bordeaux, similar to Versailles with its manicured lawns and quiet splendor, boasts examples of other architectural styles. At 4263 Bordeaux you'll see a fine example of an English Tudor home, with a well-balanced mixture of materials. Hal Thomson lived for a time in the home he designed at 4241, now torn down. And a style popular in the late thirties and forties is found at 4242 Bordeaux, a variation of the Monterey Revival called Creole Revival. The upstairs balcony is reminiscent of early New Orleans.

Continuing east on Bordeaux, you'll see a large Tudor home at 4209 Bordeaux, the first residence off Preston. The developers tended to place impressive showplace homes such as this one on larger lots along Preston where they could be seen by passersby, in hopes of attracting other wealthy residents to Highland Park West. The neighborhood soon became as sought after as any in Dallas, and has been cited as rivaling Swiss Avenue in its collection of early twentieth-century architecture. This particular home, designed by Hal Thomson, was built for $30,000 in 1924, making it one of the oldest in Highland Park West. Thomson also designed several of the most outstanding homes on Armstrong Parkway and in the Volk Estates, as well as one considered by many to be among the most impressive on Swiss Avenue. Thomson's homes, like those of Anton Korn, who also designed many Park Cities showplaces, are usually houses of large proportions that give a stately appearance to the neighborhood.

You may return to Versailles along any path you choose, as you'll find all the streets here equally appealing to the senses. You'll see a variety of architectural styles along the way, no matter how you go. Armstrong is probably a more enjoyable route north to Versailles than Douglas, however, since it is less traveled and thus quieter and will afford you the serenity to enjoy the unique sights and sounds in this community cited by architect Frank Lloyd Wright as "one of the most beautiful in the world."

As you find your way back to Flippen Park and rest upon a bench, perhaps you, too, will come to the conclusion: "Once more a perfect morn!"

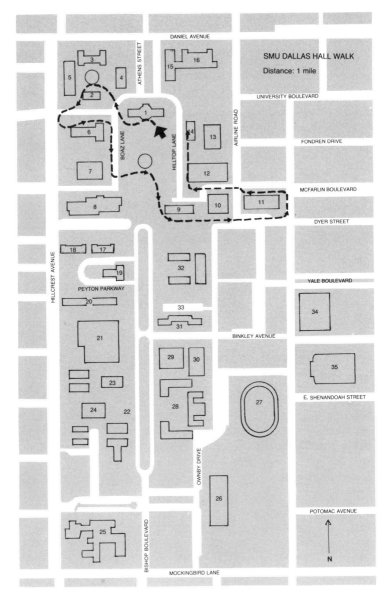

SMU DALLAS HALL WALK
Distance: 1 mile

1 Dallas Hall
2 Florence Hall
3 Storey Hall
4 Lawyers Inn
5 Underwood Law Library
6 Perkins Administration
7 McFarlin Auditorium
8 Umphrey Lee Center
9 Clements Hall
10 Hughes-Trigg Student Center
11 Patterson Hall
12 Fondren Library
13 Science Information Center
14 Hyer Hall
15 Heroy Hall
16 Fondren Science Building
17 Snider Hall
18 Virginia Hall
19 Health Center
20 Dormitories
21 Owen Arts Center
22 Perkins School of Theology
23 Bridwell Library
24 Perkins Chapel
25 Highland Park Methodist Church
26 Ownby Stadium
27 Morrison-Bell Track
28 Dormitories
29 Perkins Natatorium
30 Pool
31 Boaz Hall
32 Cox School of Business
33 Visitor Parking Lot
34 SMU Parking Garage
35 Moody Coliseum

SMU Dallas Hall Walk

UPON TAKING this walk, you will not remain untouched, for you'll have at least a passing acquaintance with a giant among men. Occasionally throughout history leaders appear who are remarkable for their vision of things to come. Combine that vision with the determination to work toward its accomplishment, add a good sense of timing and a little luck, and the result can be dramatic.

Dr. Robert S. Hyer, the first president of Southern Methodist University, channeled all of his remarkable talents toward the goal of establishing, not just a great *Methodist* university, but a great *university*, one that would stand the challenge of time. In the face of difficulties that often must have seemed insurmountable, he held fast to his dreams, even when others said it couldn't be done. Knowing that his goal was worth the effort, Hyer continued to pursue it and has left a timeless legacy for generations to come.

SMU's first yearbook, the 1916 *Rotunda*, was dedicated to Dr. Hyer, whom the students called "a gentlemanly scholar and a consistent friend." The *Rotunda* stated, "Some folks said it couldn't be done, others said it wouldn't be done, but there were those who said it would and could and should be done. And they did it."

Traveler's Advisory

Parking on the SMU campus can be a problem. You may want to schedule your visit on a weekend, or after 5:00 P.M. on a weekday, when restrictions are lifted in some of the parking areas. Read the signs, however, because some areas are restricted twenty-four hours a day. There are a few visitor parking spaces on University just inside the gates to the campus on Hillcrest. You may have better luck parking off campus, on the other side of Hillcrest, and walking into the campus on University to Dallas Hall. Be sure to note any posted restrictions on off-campus parking as well.

Weekdays only, 7:00 A.M.–11:00 P.M., parking is available in the SMU Parking Garage at the intersection of Yale and Airline, east of campus; a shuttle bus leaves the parking garage on each hour and twenty and forty minutes after the hour.

And if you don't mind walking some distance to get to Dallas Hall, there is a free visitor lot off Ownby, just north of Binkley, between Boaz Hall and Crow Hall (see the map; enter the campus via Bishop Boulevard, off Mockingbird Lane, to get to this lot, and follow posted instructions).

For additional information, call the SMU Department of Public Safety, 692-3333.

SMU Dallas Hall Walk

PICTURE A FIELD of Johnson grass stretching for miles, with an occasional rabbit scampering by and not a tree or bush in sight. Plodding across this field amidst the hum of katydids in the heat of August, 1915, are students arriving for the first time at Southern Methodist University, one by one, from all over North Texas, often raising clouds of grasshoppers as they walk. They see several hastily built dormitories (which would burn down within the next few years). But looming on the horizon is Dallas Hall, the magnificent copper-domed replica of Thomas Jefferson's ro-

In the early years of SMU, Dallas Hall housed the entire university. Peeking over the building is the top of the water tower. The Johnson grass has been raked into windrows to be baled as hay. *Courtesy of the SMU Archives*

tunda at the University of Virginia, sitting in the middle of this prairie. It must have been an awesome sight.

For several years Dallas Hall would house the entire university—its classrooms, library, administrative offices, chapel, bank, bookstore, barbershop, laboratory, and one small office for the thirty-six faculty members. About 300 students had been expected to enroll, but the eventual total was 706. Because the students kept pouring in on that first day, registration was chaotic. The ground floor of Dallas Hall first had to be cleared of all the bales of cotton that had been stored there, for in this war year some benefactors who had made financial pledges had been unable to sell their cotton and the university had accepted it in lieu of the money. The start of classes had to be delayed, and more professors had to be found. Those present on that first crazy day would have been astonished by the new computerized registration system SMU adopted in 1985— or is that chaotic in its own way today?

Begin your walk in front of Dallas Hall, at the north end of the main quadrangle of the SMU campus, and climb the steps of the building. This imposing Georgian

117

Revival–style structure with its fluted Corinthian columns is even more amazing when you realize that there were no roads to the building site. A railroad spur had to be built from the Katy line near Mockingbird to bring in the Indiana limestone columns and other materials. Dr. Robert S. Hyer, first president of SMU, was determined that it would be a first-class university. In 1912 when he drove his family to this hill and announced that this would be the site of Dallas Hall, Mrs. Hyer burst into tears. She said he couldn't possibly build a university in the middle of a prairie. But Hyer had the foresight to hire the architectural firm of Shepley, Rutan, and Coolidge, who had already designed Stanford University and the University of Chicago, and he was determined that SMU should have one great building as the crowning feature of the campus. That his great vision was a success can be affirmed by the markers you see outside the entrance to the building. In 1978 Dallas Hall received the first plaque in the Park Cities from the National Register of Historic Places. Not only is this a high honor, but it guarantees a measure of protection and qualifies it for grants and aid for restoration. And in 1979 Dallas Hall received a Texas historic marker.

Step inside the building. Dallas Hall has the most dramatic interior of any building on campus. This three-story rotunda with two wings has 53,785 square feet and is now occupied by Dedman College, the school of humanities and sciences. The copper dome has a skylight filled with stained glass wreathed with acanthus leaves. The dome rests on a brick drum, which is supported by a brick octagon with Palladian windows. The funds to build this focal point of the campus were donated solely by the citizens of Dallas, and from all denominations, not just Methodists.

Back outside, in front of Dallas Hall you'll see a sundial. If you can shoo away the local mockingbird who uses it as his personal perch, notice the appropriate inscription on the sundial, which was the gift of SMU's first graduating class in 1916. It became customary for each graduating class to donate a gift to SMU. This gift was accidentally wiped out only a year later and had to be replaced when an absent-minded professor forgot to stop in time as he drove his car up the bumpy road leading to Dallas Hall.

Turn and look at the campus around you and to the south. In 1980 ten buildings on this 164-acre campus were entered in the National Register of Historic Places as a group for their unified building theme. They are built in the Georgian Revival style with similar materials, scale, and ornament, with red brick, white trim, stone details, pedimented entry porticoes, and multipane windows. In addition to Dallas Hall, which had already been listed in the register the year before, the designated Thematic Group included nine other buildings: on your right, from south to north, you can see McFarlin Auditorium, Perkins Hall, and Florence Hall; on your left is Hyer Hall, and farther south are Clements Hall and Patterson Hall to its east; Snider Hall and Virginia Hall are among the dormitories across from the old student center (south of McFarlin Auditorium); and even Ownby Stadium is included. You'll see the last three structures on the SMU Adolescent Years Walk, and the others on this walk.

Head northwest to the law complex that includes Florence Hall, Storey Hall, Lawyers Inn, and the Underwood Law Library. (Names in parentheses in the following text indicate the architects.) Florence Hall, with its arched second-story windows, was built in 1924 as Kirby Hall (DeWitt and Lemmon), and was renamed Fred Florence Hall at the request of Karl Hoblitzelle, who contributed funds for its remodeling, completed in 1951. (See the Volk Estates Walk for more about Fred Florence, and the Preston Road–YMCA Walk for more about Karl Hoblitzelle.) Be sure to sit for a while in the Umphrey Lee Tempietto, the cenotaph in the center of the complex dedicated in memory of SMU's fourth president, and read the inscriptions. On the north side of the complex is Storey Hall (Mark Lemmon), named for Robert G. Storey, who was dean of the SMU Law School at the time the building was built. Notice the plaque on the building dated 1952. Lawyers Inn, a residence hall built in 1951, and the Underwood Law Library, built in 1971, complete the complex.

Take the covered walkway around the west end of Florence Hall and walk south and then west toward University and Hillcrest. You'll find the date 1922 on the pillars at the gateway leading into the campus at University. There was no transportation to campus, so SMU agreed to fund an extension of the trolley line in Highland Park. The "Dinkey," as it was called, came all the way out to University along the SMU side of Hillcrest, then turned around and headed back. The trolley tracks are still there, buried under the pavement. Transportation it was, but often unre-

Taken near McFarlin and Hillcrest, this picture of the "Dinkey" (so called because it was not much larger than a station wagon) shows SMU bursar Frank Reedy and driver "Dad" Johnson, a retired Dallas Railway System conductor. The sign in the distance advertises lots for sale in University Park. *Courtesy of the First RepublicBank Park Cities*

liable, for with or without help it would often jump its tracks, jolting its passengers from their seats. Greasing the tracks and similar pranks were not unusual, giving the students an excuse for being late to class.

In the grove of trees just south of the two pillars at University and Hillcrest, you'll find a surprisingly peaceful spot. Located here is a World War I memorial placed by the graduating class of 1924 in memory of the eleven SMU war veterans who gave their lives. Where the law complex now stands once grew eleven trees, planted in memory of these veterans.

Walk east on University, back toward the center of campus. Perkins Hall of Administration (DeWitt and Washburn), a four-story building with Corinthian pilasters, will be on your right, just east of the war memorial. On the first day that SMU opened there was nothing but a pile of baled hay on the site where Perkins is today.

At the east end of Perkins Hall, turn and walk south. You'll pass McFarlin Auditorium (R. H. Hunt), a massive three-story building with a grand entry stairway leading to

SMU's first president Hyer is shown dedicating the memorial marker given by the 1924 graduating class in memory of the eleven SMU students killed in World War I. The men in uniform are members of the SMU Mustang Band. *Courtesy of the SMU Magazine*

an entry with two Doric columns and Corinthian pilasters. Above are the dates 1924 and 1925. At that time it was the school's most expensive edifice, costing over $486,000. The auditorium was funded by Mr. and Mrs. R. M. McFarlin of San Antonio, and later endowed with $1 million by the McFarlin daughters. It is one of the finest college auditoriums in the U.S., and numerous academic and cultural events are staged here for the campus and surrounding communities. Third SMU president Charles C. Selecman renamed Roberts Boulevard to McFarlin Boulevard, unwittingly angering a former SMU benefactor who promptly withdrew $100,000 slated to go to SMU.

Walk over to the fountain in the center of the campus. As you can tell from the markers around it, Kennemer Fountain was originally constructed through the efforts of the classes of 1935 and 1936 and the Mothers' Club of 1936. With the help of the class of 1980 it has been rebuilt and recently named in memory of Hoyt G. Kennemer, a former SMU vice president.

Walk south from the fountain toward the flagpole, given

by the second graduating class in 1917. You'll come to a circular paved area with benches in front of a curved wall bearing the sign for Dedman College, the school of humanities and sciences. This school is named in honor of Robert H. and Nancy Dedman, who in 1981 gave an endowment of $25 million for liberal arts education at SMU.

Turn left at the flagpole and walk east past the front (the south side) of Clements Hall, where you'll find another 1980 National Register marker. This building was originally called Atkins Hall (Shepley, Rutan, and Coolidge), a women's dormitory housing 125. For the first three years after SMU opened, President Hyer and his family lived here in their own suite of rooms. Mrs. Hyer was a highly cultured southern lady who helped to set the moral tone for the women. To fully understand what this meant, it might help to briefly step back in time.

With the coming of the railroads in the 1870s, Dallas quickly became the number one distributing center in Texas for cotton buyers. At times there would be five thousand bales of cotton on Dallas's streets at once. The city then began to grow so rapidly and lustily that there was constant warfare between Dallas's solid citizens and the gamblers and outlaws. By the turn of the century this battle had largely been won in favor of law and order. Telephones, paved roads, movies, and cars were all newcomers in a rapidly changing society. Etiquette was much stricter then. Gentlemen did not spit in company and a lady never smoked or drank. Women would not even be allowed to vote until 1920.

Now picture the types of rules enforced in the dorms in those days. On rare occasions a group (never just one couple) might be given special permission to go downtown to the Majestic Theatre on a Sunday afternoon. But a woman caught chewing gum in public was restricted to campus for a short time, and a woman who had dinner alone with a man downtown was "campused" for the rest of the year! Apparently even Mrs. Hyer got in trouble for allowing the girls to dance with one another in the dormitory living room. So, with the encouragement of the strict Methodists, after three years the Hyers moved from this building to their home located near the intersection of Daniel and Hillcrest where they had a small dairy farm.

Continue east past the new Hughes-Trigg Student Center. This building is a monument to a true love story.

Mr. Trigg met his wife on campus in the very spot where it is located, and when he donated the money for the building he requested that it be built in that same place.

Farther east on Dyer Street, Patterson Hall (Coburn and Smith) was built as a heating and cooling plant in 1928. It is included in the group of buildings listed in the National Register of Historic Places in 1980.

Turn left at Airline and walk north toward McFarlin to see a remnant of the original SMU artesian well, one of three in University Park. In 1915 SMU requested that an artesian well be drilled near where the University Park City Hall is today. The water was so hot when it came out of the ground that it had to be cooled in louvered towers before use. The water was pumped from there to SMU, and Dallas Hall never needed a hot-water heater in those early years. By 1924 when University Park was incorporated there were so many people that two more wells were necessary. One of these was drilled here at Airline and McFarlin to a depth of 2,999 feet to serve SMU. Near this intersection you'll see the remains of the concrete collection bottom on which wood louvered sides permitted the water to cool. After cooling, the water was pumped either directly to the users or to the elevated storage tank behind Dallas Hall, the highest point on campus. One student recalls that as a freshman he and some friends climbed and painted that elevated water tower as a prank.

Later the water tower was moved behind Patterson Hall. Anyone who has ever moved anything very heavy realizes what a job it would be to move an elevated storage tank. The workmen jacked it up, putting crossties under it and using rolling pipes to move the unwieldy object. It was very heavy and awkward to move, the men were having a terrible time, and they began to worry that it would tip over. Just then a terrific windstorm came up and the men scattered, muttering about their luck. After the storm the workmen returned, scratching their heads and wondering what miracle had kept the tower from blowing down. About that time another man ambled up, announcing that he had gotten a message the other day to drain the storage tank. When would they like for him to do the job?

By 1934 three artesian wells could no longer provide enough water to serve SMU and the rapidly growing city of University Park, so the University Park city fathers began purchasing water from Dallas. By 1947 the Park Cities formed their own water district which now dispenses water to SMU. The old SMU water tower behind Patterson Hall was eventually taken down, and soon the water tower near Daniel Cemetery will be replaced with a much larger tank.

Turn left at McFarlin and walk west. On your right you'll be approaching the back of the Fondren Library. Fondren Library (Roscoe DeWitt) was built in the war year of 1940, the year after compulsory chapel attendance was abolished. This was the first air-conditioned building on campus. The railroad spur that had brought building materials for the construction of Dallas Hall branched off from the Katy line near Mockingbird, went behind what is now the engineering building, and stopped where Fondren Library is today. Railroads had to have a bill of lading, and there was no town nearby, so the railroad spur was named SO METH UN. This name, found on early maps, was thus the first name for University Park.

SMU actually has a whole system of libraries. Fondren East is the general library; nearby is the Science Information Center (O'Neil Ford and Arch Swank), built in 1961, housing the science and engineering library; and Fondren West or Fikes Hall houses special collections such as the DeGolyer Collection. In addition each school has its own library. In all, the system houses over two million books.

Continue to the front of the library, turn right, and walk north to your last stop, Hyer Hall (C. D. Hill and Co.). This building, located east of Dallas Hall, also has one of the 1980 National Register plaques. To the north you can see the Fondren Science Building (Mark Lemmon), built in 1950, with its white tower.

Hyer Hall is named for one of the greatest men in the history of University Park, Robert S. Hyer. The story of how SMU came to be located in Dallas and how Hyer became president of SMU is an interesting one. At the turn of the century one of the greatest shortcomings of the young city of Dallas was its lack of a first-rate university. In 1907 John Armstrong had offered a hundred acres from what is now Highland Park West for a Presbyterian university, but it never materialized. (Just think, SMU could have been located in Highland Park and called PU!) The Dallas Chamber of Commerce tried but failed to lure the Methodist university at Georgetown, Southwestern University, to Dallas.

Then the Methodists decided to create a new university, and the Dallas city fathers were determined that it should be located in Dallas, not Fort Worth.

By 1908 John Armstrong had died, but his widow donated a hundred acres of the present campus. Alex Sanger, mercantile magnate, and R. S. Munger, manufacturer and real estate holder, also donated money and land. But the greatest single gift came from W. W. Caruth, Sr., son of pioneer William Caruth, who, although he had doubts about the venture, donated sixty-eight acres of adjacent property, plus one-half interest in more than seven hundred acres—over a section of land. So by 1911 the Methodists had agreed that the new university should be located in Dallas.

The Methodists elected a Georgetown man with unusual foresight as the first president of SMU, the talented president of Southwestern University from 1898 to 1911, Robert S. Hyer. In addition to being an outstanding administrator he was also a scientist in his own right. Hyer was a physicist who, independent of Marconi experimenting with the wireless in Europe, set up the first wireless station in Texas in 1904 and sent its first wireless message, from Georgetown to Austin.

As first president of SMU, Hyer brought an enthusiasm for the project that would make the dream of SMU a reality. He was involved with every aspect of its development, from the raising of funds to approving architectural plans, recruiting a diverse faculty of brilliant scholars and persuading them to come to a university that was still a field of weeds, starting a library, acquiring laboratory equipment, and developing a curriculum. He charted the direction and quality of SMU and was determined that it would be a great university. In 1920 he became president emeritus and was a professor of physics until he died in 1929. Because he wanted a place to work he urged SMU to build a science building, though not necessarily to name it for him, and by 1926 Hyer Hall was completed.

SMU has grown and prospered since those exciting early years. As you can see from the landscaping around you, the Johnson grass has been tamed, but Dallas Hall remains the focal point of the campus and a constant reminder of Robert S. Hyer's remarkable vision.

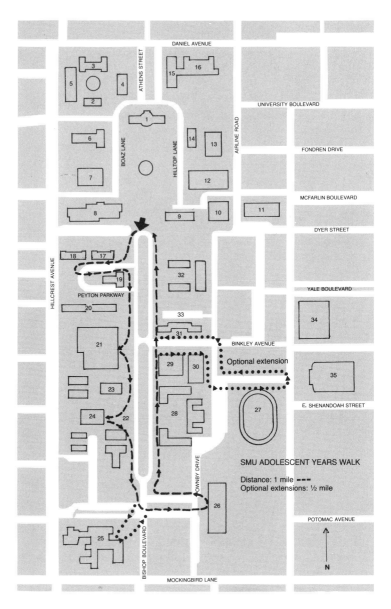

1 Dallas Hall
2 Florence Hall
3 Storey Hall
4 Lawyers Inn
5 Underwood Law Library
6 Perkins Administration
7 McFarlin Auditorium
8 Umphrey Lee Center
9 Clements Hall
10 Hughes-Trigg Student Center
11 Patterson Hall
12 Fondren Library
13 Science Information Center
14 Hyer Hall
15 Heroy Hall
16 Fondren Science Building
17 Snider Hall
18 Virginia Hall

19 Health Center
20 Dormitories
21 Owen Arts Center
22 Perkins School of Theology
23 Bridwell Library
24 Perkins Chapel
25 Highland Park Methodist Church
26 Ownby Stadium
27 Morrison-Bell Track
28 Dormitories
29 Perkins Natatorium
30 Pool
31 Boaz Hall
32 Cox School of Business
33 Visitor Parking Lot
34 SMU Parking Garage
35 Moody Coliseum

SMU Adolescent Years Walk

Southern Methodist University is a reality. It has seen its first homesick freshman arrive and go through the grind; it has seen mid-terms and finals; it has seen precedents established. It will be the privilege of posterity to hang over the railing of the Rotunda in Dallas Hall, but we did it first! Posterity can never see the first tree planted, the first plough uprooting the waving Johnson grass, the first issue of the Dinkey *and all the other things that have gone to make this first year memorable.*

—1916 *Rotunda*, SMU's yearbook

TIMES HAVE changed since the days of compulsory chapel attendance in McFarlin Auditorium and the last 11 P.M. journey of the "Dinkey" trolley returning students to the campus after a date in Dallas. The last issue of the *Dinkey*, the April Fool's Day student tabloid named for the little streetcar, appeared in 1929. But year in and year out, generations of "Mustangs" cram for finals and gather in the student center, rushing past Dallas Hall without a thought as to the sights the elegant old building has witnessed over and over again. The faces change, scandals and studies and sweethearts change, but more than seventy years later, homesick freshmen continue to enter the halls of SMU to make their mark upon its history and to emerge with the eager assurance that the future is theirs.

Traveler's Advisory

As noted for the previous walk, parking on the SMU campus can be a problem. The free visitor lot off Ownby, just north of Binkley, between Boaz Hall and Crow Hall, is reasonably convenient to the start of this walk (see the map; enter the campus via Bishop Boulevard, off Mockingbird Lane, to get to this lot, and follow posted instructions). Weekdays only, 7:00 A.M.– 11:00 P.M., parking is also available in the SMU Parking Garage at the intersection of Yale and Airline, east of campus; a shuttle bus leaves the parking garage on each hour and twenty and forty minutes after the hour.

Or you may want to schedule your visit on a weekend or after 5.00 P.M. on a weekday, when restrictions are lifted in some parking areas. Do read the signs, though, because some areas are restricted twenty-four hours a day.

For additional information, call the SMU Department of Public Safety, 692-3333.

SMU Adolescent Years Walk

IN THE WORLD of universities, SMU is a relative youngster, a newcomer on the scene. Because of the timeless Georgian architectural style used throughout the campus, SMU appears to be hundreds of years old when in reality it is only an adolescent. It is the youngest of the four private Southwest Conference schools, and a mere baby in comparison to the granddaddy of all U.S. schools, Harvard, founded 350 years ago. Even Stanford, a relative newcomer, is over a hundred years old, yet SMU only celebrated its seventy-fifth anniversary in 1986.

In that short time since the Methodists founded SMU in 1911, it has grown tremendously and overcome countless hurdles. Finances were always a struggle, for even though many donors made SMU possible, there was not a Leland Stanford who would come forward with $20 million and fund the entire project (in memory of his son), as had happened in the case of Stanford University. So every SMU president has been faced with the challenge of searching for funding for buildings and endowments to run the university, during lean times as well as good times. During the Depression most of SMU's half interest in the Caruth properties (see the Dallas Hall Walk) had to be sold to provide operating funds and faculty salaries.

The challenges have been enormous, but ways were found to solve problems and to grow in the traditions of excellence instilled by SMU's first president, Robert S. Hyer. A walk around the south end of the campus will illustrate some of the difficulties, expected as well as unexpected, that were encountered through the years.

Begin your walk at the north end of Bishop Boulevard, in the center of campus, at the flagpole donated by the second graduating class in 1917. Walking south from the flagpole, on the right side of Bishop you'll see a complex of

SMU as it was in the early forties can be seen in the distance as the Missouri-Kansas-Texas #379 Train no. 2 "Texas Special" speeds by northbound, approaching the Greenville Avenue overpass. This particular day the train had a "pusher" because it was over ten cars long. *Courtesy of the DeGolyer Library, SMU*

dormitories. Turn right to walk west into the quadrangle, past the front of Snider Hall. One tremendous problem that continued to plague the first presidents was the toll that fire took of most of the first buildings on campus. In 1926 three dorms were destroyed by fire. During the blaze, University Park's new $10,000 fire engine got stuck in the mud and also burned! Snider Hall and Virginia Hall, on your right, had to be hastily built to house the homeless students.

Third SMU president Charles C. Selecman persuaded C. W. Snider to fund one of the badly needed buildings. When Snider arrived at SMU to visit his daughter and attend the groundbreaking ceremony for Snider Hall, he decided to buy some land owned by the Daniel family and invest with Mayor J. Fred Smith of University Park in developing what is today Snider Plaza. In 1980 Snider Hall and Virginia Hall were included in the Thematic Group of ten SMU buildings to be listed in the National Register of Historic Places. As you can see, they were constructed in the Georgian Revival style to match the rest of the campus. While the buildings are very much alike, notice that Snider Hall has Ionic columns and Virginia Hall has Corinthian ones. The roof details are also different. The three other dorms in this complex were built in the 1950s.

Retrace your steps to Bishop Boulevard and continue south past the Memorial Health Center, built in 1960. Notice the inscriptions in the arched marble insets on both sides of the door. The health center could have been used during another crisis, the 1917–1918 flu epidemic which caused 37 percent of all deaths in Texas that year. At this same time, World War I was also taking its toll of students.

But through these and other crises the construction of new buildings on the campus has continued steadily, and academic programs have expanded as well. In 1915 SMU offered three degrees, but today an undergraduate is offered seventy-five fields of study. This growth would not have been possible without continuing generous gifts from SMU's supporters.

Continue south past the dormitory complex to the Owen Art Center. This building, which houses the university's music, art, and drama facilities, was designed by architect George Dahl, who coordinated the efforts of the army of architects that designed the twenty-six buildings at Fair Park for the 1936 Centennial Exposition. Various sculpture

Fire was a grim reaper of many early SMU buildings, as shown on this page from the 1926 *Rotunda*, SMU's yearbook. Three men's dorms were destroyed, and during the blaze University Park's new $10,000 fire engine got stuck in the mud and burned, too. *Courtesy of the SMU Archives*

stands in front of the building. You can read more about this center and the Owen family for whom it is named on the walls by the entrances on each side. In the central courtyard is a sculpture by Maillol, a French sculptor.

On the north side of the courtyard is the Meadows Museum, made possible by a gift from Algur H. Meadows in the 1960s, in memory of his wife, Virginia. The Meadows Museum houses the finest collection of Spanish art outside of Spain. See this collection Monday-Saturday 10:00 A.M.– 5:00 P.M. and Sunday 1:00–5:00 P.M. The music school and the fine arts programs were absorbed by the new Meadows School of the Arts, which Meadows then endowed with the stunning sum of $30 million. Funds for the Bob Hope Theatre were donated by the comedian himself, and Caruth Auditorium, which by the way is acoustically perfect, is named for the Caruth family which has been so generous to SMU.

Continue south on Bishop Boulevard to one of the loveliest complexes on campus, the $3.5 million Perkins School of Theology. Dedicated in 1951, it consists of seven Georgian-style buildings designed by Mark Lemmon and spread on 16 acres of the 164-acre SMU campus. The theology school was one of SMU's first three schools (the other two were music and liberal arts). A 1914 map of the campus shows a creek cutting diagonally across the campus and winding down through Arden Forest (better known as Ardent Forest because it was a refuge where lovers could hold hands on campus), also known as Perkins Grove, where you're standing now. This creek resurfaced in Highland Park into what is called Hackberry Creek. In the center of this complex is Perkins Chapel, with its serene interior. Read the marker in the brick walkway in front of the chapel before you go inside. On the north side of the complex is Bridwell Library with its rare book collection. Brick walkways tie the whole complex together.

While the Perkins complex is evidence of the strong religious beliefs of the founding Methodists, first president Robert S. Hyer insisted from the outset that intellectual freedom should be maintained at SMU. A devoutly religious man, he still felt that divergent ideas should be heard. Thus the stage was set for numerous conflicts in which his belief has been tested again and again. Once an English professor wrote the introduction for a story by a then little-known writer, William Faulkner, a story some felt was immoral in tone. Some called for the professor's resignation, while others defended him. The debate was hot and heavy, but academic freedom finally won out and he was allowed to stay.

Another example of that commitment to the freedom of ideas occurred in the early 1950s when black students enrolled in Perkins School of Theology, and later in other SMU schools, long before any other university in Texas was integrated. In the late fifties President Willis Tate and the university stood up to McCarthy-like attacks, maintaining their climate of freedom. Tate believed that a nation is free only as long as universities remain free in their quest for truth. His was not a popular position in those days, but he had the courage to defend it.

The Highland Park United Methodist Church, organized in 1915, met in homes until this building, known affectionately as the "Little Brown Church," was completed at Mockingbird and Hillcrest. *Courtesy of the DeGolyer Library, SMU*

As you continue south on Bishop Boulevard, you can see in the distance on Mockingbird Lane the Highland Park United Methodist Church, which is not part of the campus. You might want to extend your walk and loop over by the church to get a closer look. (If not, read the following paragraph and continue.) The history of SMU and the church are closely intertwined. The Methodists founded SMU and later SMU helped to found this church by giving it land to build on, deeding to the church a corner of the hundred acres donated by Mrs. John Armstrong. In 1916 a small, barnlike brown frame church was begun. When completed it stood in lonely, grassy fields with "No Hunting" signs nearby. A long boardwalk was constructed from the front door of this church across the fields to Dallas Hall. But the walkway became the home of hundreds of wasps, and not a few early worshippers sat through services with swollen eyes or hands. During the twenties, money was set aside for a new church with the help of SMU president Selecman and the Methodist Board, and in 1926 the present Gothic sanctuary with its massive tower was built, being updated in 1972. The architect was Mark Lemmon, who designed the Highland Park Presbyterian Church and many buildings on the SMU campus, and also had a part in designing the Hall of State at Fair Park. The church's pastor from 1923 to 1936 was Umphrey Lee, a great orator known for his short, pithy sermons, who would later be a popular SMU president. This church now has one of the largest congregations of any Methodist church in the United States and even in the world, so large that in the past many Easter services have been held at Moody Coliseum.

At the corner of the parking lot north of the church, cross to the east side of Bishop Boulevard and take the wide walkway leading between two rows of oak trees to walk east to Ownby Stadium. The southern end of campus where Bishop Boulevard runs today once was a nine-hole golf course built by a group of faculty and staff members in 1920. This was the year that Hyer resigned and second president Hiram A. Boaz launched a successful million-dollar fund-raising campaign.

One of the earliest clashes on campus came in the early twenties when SMU decided to recruit a winning football team. The story actually begins in 1915 when Ray Morrison, a football coach, was hired—but for the position of YMCA secretary because bursar Frank Reedy knew President Hyer preferred croquet to football. When Hyer met Morrison for the first time, he said there would be no YMCA program and suggested Morrison teach Latin or math. Morrison was given a trigonometry class, which upset him because he wanted to coach, so he often let someone else do the teaching. Soon Morrison was asked to start a football team, in spite of Hyer, and became SMU's first athletic coach at a salary of $2,000 a year. Morrison got some mules to scrape away the Johnson grass, then sodded the field with Bermuda grass dug up along Airline Road. On the first day of practice nobody knew how to pass, so Coach Morrison threw to all the boys. After about ten minutes somebody finally caught the ball and everybody cheered. That first season the players were nearly killed during their games, and the second wasn't much better. Rice beat the Mustangs 146–3.

It's no wonder that talk began about recruiting a winning football team, so a great debate began on campus over priorities. The Mustangs went from a 1–5 record in 1921 to a 6-3-1 record in 1922. Still the debate raged. The faculty athletic committee stated that the function of the university was not to provide a spectacle for entertaining crowds but to interest as many students as possible in healthful sports. But 1923 was an immortal year, for SMU won their first Southwest Conference football championship. By then their coach was "Matty" Bell. (Later in this walk an optional side trip will take you to the Morrison-Bell Track, named in honor of these two coaches, which is located at the site of the first football field.)

The championship team needed a stadium, so SMU borrowed $175,000 to build it, settling any questions about SMU's priorities. J. C. Ownby and father donated $10,000 for the grounds around the stadium.

When you reach the stadium, you'll see on your right the statue of a horse. SMU's first mascot, the first Peruna, is buried here. Robert S. Hyer himself had chosen Harvard red and Yale blue as SMU's colors, but his secretary chose the mascot. She looked out at Morrison's early football players and remarked that they looked like a bunch of wild mustangs. Peruna was a patent medicine, a potent elixir, so they used that name for their first Mustang, hoping he would be a strong good-luck charm. The original Peruna debuted in 1932 but died in 1934 when he escaped from some Aggies who had captured him and was hit by a car

In 1935 the SMU Mustang football team won the national championship. *Courtesy of the SMU Archives*

on Mockingbird Lane. The second Peruna must have had more magic, because in 1935 the Mustangs won the national championship. The marker by the statue also mentions Perunas II, III, and IV, the 1947–48 championship mascot. That year Doak Walker became the only SMU football player ever to receive the Heisman Trophy. Notice also the bronze plaques dated 1926, 1982, and 1985.

By World War II the football team was well established. There were dozens of new buildings as well as fraternity and sorority houses, popular fourth president Umphrey Lee was chosen, and there seemed to be a mood of optimism on campus. In 1939 compulsory chapel attendance was abolished and SMU hosted its first legitimate all-school dance. That happy time was needed, for after World War II SMU would go through such dramatic, drastic changes that it would never be the same.

Walk back to Bishop Boulevard, turn right, and continue north. On the east side of Bishop you'll see an open field and a dormitory complex north of the field. Before the war this whole area was still open fields, intramural athletic fields, and baseball diamonds, but almost overnight they seemed to fill with trailers to house the thousands of GI's returning home intent upon seeking a higher education. This part of the campus was called Trailerville. The students who lived in those trailers would have envied the many dorms standing here today.

Before the war the largest student body had numbered less than four thousand. During each of the four years after the war, enrollment exceeded ten thousand. Fourth president Lee met this challenge head on and in 1946 began a program that would add thirty-six major buildings for about $20 million. Classes were held six days a week, some starting at dawn and others lasting until late at night, twelve months a year. Faculty members were recruited wherever they could be found. No longer was there time for leisurely golf games on campus. President Lee led SMU through this period of greatest crisis of its youth and ushered it into a new age. Since World War II more than sixty buildings have been added to the campus.

This period of growth continued under fifth president Willis Tate, who initiated most of SMU's doctoral programs. Believing the well-educated person is a whole human being, he worked for requiring all students to enroll in a series of liberal arts courses before concentrating on their majors, a policy that continues today. One of his greatest accomplishments was to win the support of a large core of Dallas citizens who would fund new buildings, programs, and endowments, such as the Meadows School. This trend of increased support by local citizens can be seen in the latest additions to this continually growing campus.

North of the dormitory complex you'll pass the Perkins Natatorium and outdoor pool, home of the nationally ranked swim team.

If you wish to take a side trip to see the Morrison-Bell Track, turn right on Binkley. (If not, just read the following and continue north on Bishop.) To reach the track, walk east on Binkley. Turn right on Ownby, east of the pool, and then turn left to walk along the north end of the track. In the distance across Airline Road you'll see Moody

Coliseum. When it was completed in 1956 it became SMU's largest building, now the home of the 1988 Southwest Conference basketball champions. At the corner of the track facing Airline you'll see bronze plaques set in a slab of granite, honoring Coaches Morrison and Bell.

Retrace your steps to Bishop Boulevard and continue north. On your right you'll see the Edwin L. Cox School of Business, with two new wings made possible by gifts from Trammell Crow and Cary Maguire. It is one of the most advanced business education facilities in the country, housing its own state-of-the-art computer center and telecommunications center. Take time to walk through the landscaped open courtyard. Underground are the library and lounges.

While this newest complex and a new parking garage on Airline were being built under eighth president Donald Shields, the campus was rocked with a crisis that would shake its very foundations. Rumors of improper payments to football players and infractions of NCAA rules finally were substantiated. The football squad was placed on probation in 1985. As if this weren't enough, improper payments continued for another year, at which time the NCAA suspended the 1987 football season. Other controversies on campus in past years paled before this one, which harkened back to the great debate in the twenties over the role of football in a university. Now that debate resurfaced and raged again. In 1987 the SMU Board of Governors was abolished in an attempt to restructure the university's governing bodies.

In mid-1987 after an extensive search, the ninth president of SMU was chosen, A. Kenneth Pye, a legal scholar, Roman Catholic, and former chancellor of Duke University. A story is told about the scrupulously honest Pye that one Christmas a law student sent him a crate of Florida oranges, only to have Pye return it. He is known for his ability to make unpopular changes if he feels they are needed.

Perhaps the tragedy of the improper payments and the revelations involving some of the leaders of the university will help SMU forge a new direction. Certainly SMU will learn from its mistakes and, like any adolescent, will have a chance to grow in the process. Adolescents are known for their rash, sometimes foolish, often playful behavior. But they can and do become law-abiding adults who are a credit to their community. SMU has always responded to crises, and in so doing has grown and matured. Looking at this latest crisis in the perspective of SMU's past history, filled with leaders of strong moral fiber and great vision, one cannot help but believe that SMU will emerge stronger and greater than ever as a result.

TURTLE CREEK BOULEVARD

CARUTH BOULEVARD

CARUTH PARK

HILLCREST AVENUE

COLGATE AVENUE

CITY LIMIT

Optional extension

AIRLINE ROAD

SOUTHWESTERN BOULEVARD

GREENBRIER DRIVE

CENTENARY DRIVE

WENTWOOD DRIVE

VILLANOVA DRIVE

NORTHWEST HIGHWAY

DURHAM STREET

MARQUETTE STREET

BOEDEKER STREET

ST. LAURENT PLACE

STONECOURT

CARUTH WALK

CORNERSTONE PARKWAY

CARUTH HILL

CARUTH COURT

Distance: 3 miles ---
Optional extension: 1 mile

LAKESIDE PARK

N ⟶

NORTH CENTRAL EXPRESSWAY

Caruth Walk

SOUTHERN hospitality didn't end at the Mississippi River. As pioneers came west and settled, they brought with them a spirit of camaraderie with other adventurous souls. It was the custom to give lodging and a warm welcome to any stranger who came along. He was offered the best food in the house and given the best bed for the night. He wouldn't have dreamed of insulting his host by offering to pay for such hospitality, and even small children were taught not to accept money. Pioneers were proud of their hospitality and gladly shared their homes. University Park's early settlers were no exception, evidenced, as you will see, by the pioneer Caruth family, known for their hospitality to strangers and their generosity to the new community and to the university around which it grew.

Traveler's Advisory

Weary travelers be forewarned that this is the longest walk in the book, and part of the walk is uphill. A suggested shortcut is to walk the Caruth Park portion, circling through the park and returning to your car to drive to Caruth Homeplace. So that you don't miss the feel of the walk, be sure to drive east on Southwestern to Boedeker, bearing in mind that you are in the midst of what was once the Caruth family's "Little Pasture." Turn left at Boedeker and enter Caruth Homeplace at Caruth, following the same route as the walk. Your return trip, in your car as in the walk, will be down Caruth, back toward the park.

Caruth Walk

THE STORY of University Park begins over a hundred years ago with the arrival in 1848 of William Caruth, who eventually owned forty thousand acres of land and became the largest landowner in Dallas. Riding on horseback all the way from Kentucky, he arrived with nothing but a gold watch, a hundred dollars in his pocket, and his horse. He was so impressed with this rolling prairie that he wrote back and summoned his brother, Walter, who arrived the next year. They borrowed a thousand dollars from their father and started a little store named "W. Caruth and Brother" near John Neely Bryan's cabin on the Trinity, selling everything from buggy whips to butter. Their business soon prospered, the loan was repaid, and the brothers began investing in land.

By 1854 the Caruths were dealing with banks all over the country. They opened the first real estate addition in Dallas, near Ross and McKinney, and later bought 492 acres from the Cole heirs that would eventually become the First Addition of Highland Park. But William became engrossed with the idea of growing cotton on the black, waxy soil north of Dallas, which was perfect for this crop. He began buying farms for about nine dollars an acre and created a huge plantation that extended from White Rock Creek (the lower part of which is now a lake) past Preston Road on the west, near Forest Lane on the north, and to Mockingbird Lane on the south.

Begin your walk on Turtle Creek Boulevard between Southwestern and Greenbrier, at Caruth Park. The lake you see on the southwest side of the park is part of Turtle Creek, whose headwaters can be found seven hundred feet north of Walnut Hill Lane near Hillcrest. Caruth Lake retards the flow of surface water of Turtle Creek from the north, and any overflow is carried through underground storm sewers. You can see the hole in the lake where an overflow drain takes the creek water into an underground culvert where it heads south out of sight until it converges with the lake created at Curtis Park on Lovers Lane. There it forms the tributary that flows into a lake created at Williams Park on University. The street called Turtle Creek actually used to be a flowing, meandering creek.

The land for Caruth Park was given by W. W. Caruth, Sr. (Will, the son of William Caruth) in 1929. Since this area of University Park lacked any public or commercial building, for years Caruth Park was the location of precinct political conventions, weather permitting.

Take the sidewalk past the tennis courts into the park. Notice the stonework in the picnic table as you walk across the stone bridge. Until it was bulldozed in November, 1987, there was a little stone building (formerly a restroom) that was a good example of the sandstone work done during the Depression of the 1930s by the Works Progress Administration (WPA) and paid for by Franklin Roosevelt's New Deal. In the period from 1938 to 1942 as many as a thousand WPA workers were employed by University Park, improving streets, parks, sewer and water services, and collecting garbage, for the WPA paid seventy cents of every dollar that University Park spent on the city. By 1945, with the help of the WPA, most of the paving and sewers were complete in University Park.

The tennis courts were also built during the thirties. The newer creative playground, built in 1975 and remodeled in 1986 and again in 1988, was promoted by two energetic and persistent mothers. It was the first creative playground in the Park Cities and was originally built specifically for

This WPA-built stone building stood in Caruth Park from the late 1930s until November 1987, when it was bulldozed to make way for children's play equipment. *Photo by Glenn Galloway*

ages two to five. A neighborhood Fourth of July parade and celebration has been held at Caruth Park several years.

Turn right at the playground and cross the second stone bridge to see a shallow pond that has been turned into a water garden. The park department has installed a pump to bring in water from the lake, so this pond will never go dry. The tropical water lilies and other water plants placed there by Ray Butler, a local water garden enthusiast, die out in the winter and have to be replanted each year. They begin blooming in June and last until winter.

Butler has planted more than twenty varieties of lilies, including several night-blooming plants. Among these is the "Great Victoria," a lily from South Africa whose leaves grow to a diameter of five to six feet. It is distinguished by its large flat leaves, reddish on the edges with small ripples. Other lilies include the copper-colored "Comanche" and the white night-blooming "Jackwoods White Knight," which opens at approximately 9:30 in the evening. A blue native lily was developed by Kurt Strawn of Austin. You may pass a local artist setting up an easel to paint or sketch the colorful water garden.

The flagpole at the east end of the park also displays WPA stonework. Its bronze marker, dated 1939, bears the name of Elbert Williams, fourth mayor of University Park (1938–1942). In just a few years he would dedicate Smith Park (see the Hyer-Greenbrier Walk). A newspaper article in December of 1939 boasted that the "creation of Caruth lake from a muddy water hole . . . a modern comfort station, two arched bridges having a 20 foot span and a retaining wall all constructed of choice Lewisville stone, are part of an engineering triumph."

Walk east out of the park and turn south on Hillcrest toward Southwestern. Try to imagine this area without any trees. There were a few trees by the creek, but most of this land was rolling prairie covered with Johnson grass. The Caruths cut much of it for hay, but the price was so cheap that often many acres were left standing uncut. By winter the grass was three or four feet tall and very dangerous. To prevent an unwanted fire, Will Caruth would wait for a favorable wind and set fire to it on purpose. One day they would burn from their house (near Central Expressway today) to Airline, another day from Airline to Preston. Will would shoot the rabbits that ran ahead of the fire. By the end of the day his buggy would be full—and for the next few days the menu would be full—of rabbit.

Mrs. Caruth used to consider an outing to watch the "burning" a treat. She must truly have loved the out-of-doors because she chose to go plover hunting with Will the day before they were married in 1905 rather than have her final fitting of her trousseau at Titche-Goettinger. It is appropriate that a park bears her name.

Turn left on Southwestern and walk east. The magnificent trees along Southwestern, especially stunning in their fall colors, belie the actual age of the street. It's a relative newcomer compared to Airline, Lovers Lane, and Northwest Highway. Many of these trees were planted when Southwestern was paved around 1927, just before Caruth Park was built. Southwestern runs through the area that the Caruths called the Little Pasture, where their extra horses and mules were turned out to graze. (The Big Pasture was east of what is now Central Expressway, and the North Pasture was where Hillcrest High School now stands.) Nearby was a cotton gin run by a treadmill using small mules, to serve the southern end of their plantation.

When the Little Pasture was sold off to developers, two men, J. S. Craig and H. E. Yarbrough, seemed to have a large part of the market sewed up. Yarbrough would later become the sixth mayor of University Park (1946–1950). While the rest of the country was struggling to pull itself out of the Depression during the late thirties and early forties, these builders, Craig and Yarbrough, were competing to see which could build the finer homes along Southwestern. The fruits of their labors are still visible, and the winners were the community and its new residents who benefitted from the profusion of fine homes along this busy thoroughfare.

After Dr. Umphrey Lee retired as SMU's fourth president, he moved to 3307 Southwestern, where he lived until his death. The home at 3225, built in 1935, lured Virginia Worthington to move here from her house on Lakeside Drive. Among the homes built by developers, don't miss a stately home built individually at 3205 in Tudor style. It was designed by architect Anton Korn, who also acted as the contractor to ensure that his plans were carefully carried out, a practice not uncommon for Korn. This was the first home built on Southwestern. (For more on Anton Korn, see the Connor Lake Walk.)

As you enter the 3100 block, you are in the section known as Caruth Hills, built mostly in the forties. The trees have grown over the street forming a canopy. In autumn the burnished golds, sienna browns, and varying hues from nature's palette—particularly striking in the morning or evening when the sun's rays filter through the colorful leaves—make this a walk not to miss during that season.

The area south of the corner of Southwestern and Boedeker is the part of the Little Pasture where Mrs. Caruth remembered a good-sized lake, near where Dublin crosses Bryn Mawr. She recalled duck hunting there. Another oldtimer remembers camping overnight as a youngster with friends in that area near a creek. The big old trees show that indeed there was water there, and it's likely that Dublin Street covers what used to be a creek.

Cross to the east side of Boedeker and turn left, then follow Boedeker north to Caruth Boulevard. Only in the late seventies did these homes on your right spring up. Will's son, W. W. Caruth, Jr., and the Caruth heirs are naturally concerned about preserving what remains of the homeplace and preferred to see high-quality townhomes built rather than skyscrapers.

Turn right on Caruth and walk east to Cornerstone Parkway. As you enter this new development called Caruth Homeplace through the brick pillars, you are actually in Dallas. Notice the date, Circa 1852, on the entry stone.

Turn left on Cornerstone Parkway and right on Lakeside Park. Over on the left, past a landscaped median, you'll see a bubbling fountain with benches facing it. From here you can see the Caruth mansion, now owned and occupied by George Caruth, great grandson of William Caruth. The house is easier to see in winter when the huge bois d'arc trees, planted by William, have no leaves.

When William Caruth married his wife, Mattie Worthington, in 1864, they moved into a small ranch house that was on the property when the land was purchased in 1852. It was a one-story structure built with native oak logs for joists, hand-hewn shingles, and clapboard siding. That building, still standing behind the mansion, is probably one of the oldest in Dallas County. In 1962 George remodeled it to serve as his bachelor quarters before he married.

Around 1870 the field hands began constructing the stately two-story southern mansion, known as Caruth Hill. The yellow pine lumber was hauled in from East Texas by oxen, because the railroad didn't arrive until 1872, and the

Caruth Hill was designed after houses Mattie Caruth had seen while living in Mississippi. *Courtesy of the DeGolyer Library, SMU*

bricks were hand-made. William and Mattie's son, Will, was born here and died seventy-three years later across the hall from where he was born.

Built on the highest point in the area, Caruth Hill attracted travelers on their way to Dallas, six miles to the south. It contained a "Traveler's Room," which made it renowned for its hospitality, for anyone could stay the night and have breakfast in the morning, as long as they were gone by sun-up. No questions were asked; the Caruths respected their guests' privacy. The Caruths hope others will respect their privacy today.

In 1938 remodeling began at Caruth Hill and an Ionic colonnade was added. The fountain in front of the house was bought in New Orleans around 1940. Will and his wife had both died before their historic home was awarded a Texas state historic medallion in 1963.

If you look due north through the fence you can see horses and a scattering of old barns, the remains of the once-huge plantation. A large dairy barn that burned many years ago was so enormous it could be seen all the way from Plano.

W. W. Caruth, Jr., who once had a favorite pony here named Wig, won a scholarship to SMU, graduated second in his class, and received a business degree from Harvard. He used the thousand dollars his father, Will, gave him for not smoking before he was twenty-one to start a construction business at Caruth and Greenville. Known for his many real estate additions, he is also a philanthropist, as was his father. It has been up to him to oversee the sale of these once-vast lands.

Of all the pioneer families important to the history of the Park Cities, perhaps the Caruths have had the most far-reaching influence. Not only was University Park carved out of their land, but they also once owned the land that started Highland Park. It was their generous gift of land that succeeded in drawing a major university to Dallas and helped to create SMU.

Return to Boedeker the way you entered Caruth Homeplace. As you cross Boedeker and continue west on Caruth, it's like entering another era of time. These one-story homes were built in the post–World War II baby boom era, a time of optimism before the Cold War set in. University Park was experiencing a burst of growth and houses were springing up so fast that the city had a hard time keeping up with providing water and sewer to them.

On the crest of the hill between Durham and Airline the character of Caruth Boulevard changes again as the homes become two-story with larger lot sizes. Along the parkway you can see some recently planted red oak trees. These were part of a "Trees for the Town" project whereby the neighborhood agreed to purchase trees from the city for forty dollars each, and the city planted them free in the parkway. This Park Cities community project was begun by Judge Pat Robertson of Highland Park in 1975. For more information call him at 522-2788.

Continue west on Caruth to Airline, one of the oldest roads in the county and the quickest route to Dallas in the early days. William Caruth would hitch a pair of mules to a light wagon and rush to Dallas via Airline to his store to bring home nails or whatever he needed, returning in an hour. This narrow dirt road was waxy black mud in the winter, but in the summer it was hard, smooth, and fast. At the turn of the century, Richardson Road (now Central Expressway) was a graveled road graded into ditches on the side, muddy and full of holes in the winter, dusty and full of holes in the summer.

If you wish to take an optional side trip and add a little

more than one mile to the walk, turn right on Airline and walk north toward Northwest Highway. (If not, just read the next few paragraphs and continue west on Caruth.) The Caruths had another cotton gin at the corner of Northwest Highway and what is now Hillcrest that served the north end of the plantation. Nearby was a small schoolhouse for white children. Another schoolhouse for colored children was located on Lovers Lane and Richardson Road, and was used as a church on Sundays.

At Airline and Northwest Highway the Caruth Chapel was built prior to 1870 and maintained by the Caruth brothers. It served the plantation and the surrounding territory, and various circuit riders acted as preachers. The chapel burned many years ago. Fittingly, Northway Christian Church is located on the same site. In 1955 Mrs. Will Caruth gave an altar set to the church in memory of the old chapel.

Cross to the west side of Airline at Northwest Highway and look across into the cemetery. A large gray stone bears the name Caruth and locates the private area where many Caruths are buried today. Will's daughter, Mattie Caruth Byrd, owned and ran this cemetery for many years.

Return south on Airline to Caruth, then walk west on Caruth to Hillcrest. Try to imagine this area with only a few dirt roads and no houses in sight. **Turn left on Hillcrest to return to Caruth Park,** a fitting monument to a family that generously donated this land they loved to enhance their community.

Will the monuments and landmarks we establish in our lifetime stand the test of time and serve as guideposts and inspiration to future generations? Or in our era of plastics, fads, and fast foods, will we be in too much of a hurry to stop and ponder the heritage we are leaving behind us? Will the homes we build, the parks we improve, the markers we leave be worthy of preservation? And will we have the foresight to save what is worthy of preserving? We are fortunate that Caruth Hill still stands to tell its story.

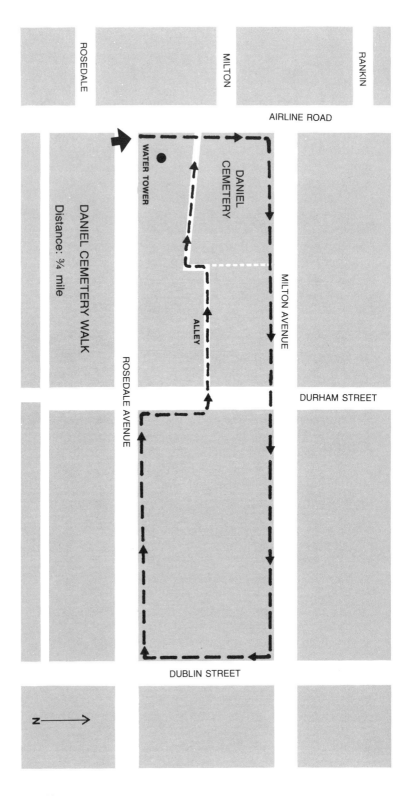

ROSEDALE

MILTON

RANKIN

AIRLINE ROAD

WATER TOWER

DANIEL CEMETERY

DANIEL CEMETERY WALK

Distance: ¾ mile

ROSEDALE AVENUE

ALLEY

MILTON AVENUE

DURHAM STREET

DUBLIN STREET

N →

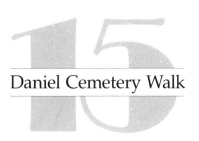

Daniel Cemetery Walk

THE OSAGE orange tree, originally found in Texas, Oklahoma, and Arkansas and named for the Osage Indians, is also called bois d'arc (bodark) or bowwood. (Bois d'arc is French for "wood of the bow.") It belongs to the mulberry family and has an inedible fruit known as horse apples or Osage oranges. But far from being useless, this tree was extremely important to the Indians and to pioneer settlers as well. It grew fast in this black soil and sometimes was used as a hedge because of its thorny twigs. Settlers "fenced" their 640-acre sections with them before barbed wire came into use, and later trimmed the trees to act as fence posts.

The yellow bois d'arc wood is tough and bug-resistant and was useful to the settlers in a number of ways. Wagon wheels were made of it, homes were built on foundation piers made of it, and streets were even paved with it in early Dallas. (By the twenties such paving had been replaced by bricks or concrete.) Bois d'arc wood was preferred by the Indians for their bows and war clubs. And a yellow dye can be made by boiling chips of the wood in water.

Bois d'arc hedges have long since lost their popularity because the trees grew so high they shaded the adjacent crops and had to be trimmed constantly, but several old fence rows still exist in the Park Cities, among these some on Lovers Lane. In the winter the numerous fox squirrels in the neighborhood often seek the fallen "oranges," feeding on the seeds within.

If you have any hungry silkworms, they'll thrive on bois d'arc leaves.

The bois d'arc tree is easy to identify even during seasons when the ground around it is not covered with the nubby green fruit. The trunk has a distinctive yellow-orange color where the bark has fallen away.

Throughout the Park Cities you'll find examples of these hardy trees, surviving far longer than the human lifespan and standing in stately silence over the community that has sprouted around them. The tales they could tell—of buffalo hunts, wagon trains, outlaws, courageous pioneers, untimely deaths, horseless carriages, and the vagaries of weather—are all sealed forever within the concentric rings of their massive trunks.

Daniel Cemetery Walk

NEARLY EVERY day hundreds of people pass within a short distance of one of the most historic places in the Park Cities, never knowing it's there. It happens to be a cemetery, the only one in the Park Cities—the family burial plot of the Daniel family, who journeyed here to the wild Texas frontier in wagons, all the way from civilized Alabama.

Frances Sims Daniel was a true Daughter of the American Revolution (DAR), for her father, William Sims, was a soldier in the Revolutionary War. Her husband, Rev. John Daniel, was an Alabama preacher, and a year after he died she bravely set out west toward the Texas frontier with six of her eight living children, her widowed sister, Mrs. Nancy Harlan, and several slaves. When they arrived in 1849, she invested her life savings in a section of land (640 acres) for fifty cents an acre. The section was bounded on the north by what is now Lovers Lane, on the south by Haynie, on the west by the "creek with all the turtles," and on the east (roughly) by the present location of Central Expressway. John Neely Bryan had built his cabin on the Trinity River just eight years earlier, and Texas had been annexed only four years earlier. In 1850 the first United States Census showed 430 inhabitants in Dallas. The Daniel family lived "out in the country" north of Dallas, and were the first inhabitants of what would become University Park.

Begin your walk at the intersection of Airline and Rosedale, near the water tower. Although there are SMU signs on it, the tower is not owned by Southern Methodist University. University Park has always owned the tower, which now provides water to the campus as well as other parts of the city. Looking south toward Daniel Avenue, the northern boundary of the SMU campus, you can see the white tower of the Fondren Science Building. Beyond that building is Dallas Hall (not visible from here) with its huge copper tower, the first building on the SMU campus, built in 1912. Frances Daniel and her family camped where Dallas Hall is now located, but were unable to find sufficient water on top of the hill to build there.

As you begin walking north on Airline, look north past the cemetery to where you see some old bois d'arc trees along Airline, across Milton. This is where Mrs. Daniel's first home and water well were located. The cemetery was originally an orchard behind the Daniel house. Many of the bois d'arcs around the cemetery were planted by Mrs. Daniel, perhaps as a fence for the orchard or cemetery, and have been there over a hundred years. At the turn of the century her daughter Margaret built the small fence around the one and one-tenth acres you see today. Max Daniel, who with his brother Bill now owns Daniel Cleaners, remembers mowing the cemetery with a hand mower as a boy, and by the time he finished it seemed more like *three* acres.

At the southwest corner of the cemetery, you'll pass a giant bois d'arc, so old it's too big to wrap your arms around. Then you'll see two pillars marking the entrance to the cemetery. The bronze marker on one pillar says "Daniel Cemetery Founded 1850." On the other pillar will soon be a Texas historic marker (dated 1988), one of only three in the Park Cities, all in University Park (the first one was the Preston Road marker near the YMCA; the second was Dallas Hall). You'll also see a Park Cities Historical Society landmark designation marker.

Go slowly north along Airline to get various views of the cemetery through the hedges. Old Frank, a slave from Alabama, was the first person to be buried here when he died in 1850. The original wooden marker that located his grave is no longer there, but he was buried in the northwest corner of the orchard, along with several other slaves. Frank must have been very old, for he had been a slave of Frances's father for many years before he was bequeathed to her at her father's death in 1813. Frances also was willed two more slaves, a colt, a saddle and bridle, her bed and other furniture, and a cow.

Frances's daughter Isabella was the first family member to be buried in the cemetery. She had married Alexander Harwood, county clerk of Dallas (for whom Harwood Street was named), but died in childbirth in 1851 at the age of fourteen. Isabella is buried in the southeast corner of the orchard where all the early white graves are located. Very few tombstones in Dallas County are dated as early as 1851. Isabella and Alexander's daughter, Fannie Belle Harwood, lived only nine years and was buried beside Isabella in 1860.

The tombstones reveal the terrible toll that the frontier took on its early inhabitants. There are many small stones marking the graves of small children and teenagers. It is hard to contemplate death, especially an untimely one.

The solemnity of this cemetery calls to mind some of the familiar lines from Thomas Gray's poem "Elegy Written in a Country Churchyard":

For them no more the blazing hearth shall burn,
Or busy housewife ply her evening care:
No children run to lisp their sire's return,
Or climb his knees the envied kiss to share. . . .

Full many a gem of purest ray serene,
The dark unfathom'd caves of ocean bear:
Full many a flower is born to blush unseen,
And waste its sweetness on the desert air.

As you approach the corner of Milton Avenue, you can get a closer look at the site of the first Daniel homestead, marked by the old bois d'arc trees on Airline.

Turn right on Milton and walk east. The row of hedges rounding the corner, the crape myrtles, cedars, and huge older trees are a haven for birds. This is an excellent place for bird watching and listening to the symphony of their myriad songs as they fly to and from their protected home. Numerous bluejays, mockingbirds, red-winged blackbirds, and cardinals defend their various territories, but all remain a respectful distance from a mischievous old crow who occasionally sits in the crook of one of the tall trees.

In this sylvan setting Frances herself was buried at the age of fifty-seven in 1853, only four years after she had arrived. A DAR marker stands beside her grave, as well as beside four other graves of her direct descendants. She can

be considered the matriarch and first pioneer settler of what is now University Park, since the Caruths did not move to their farm until 1852. (See the Caruth Walk.) Buried along with her are her sister, Mrs. Nancy Harlan, who died in 1851, and nearly ninety descendants and spouses. Several soldiers from the War with Mexico, the Civil War, and World War I are buried here, as well as five slaves. The graves in Daniel Cemetery are eloquent reminders of University Park's first residents, who now rest here in serene silence.

Cross Durham and continue east on Milton Street, enjoying the sights and sounds of today's residential neighborhood that grew up on Daniel land. At 3009 Milton is the home of Jack Kirven, former University Park city engineer (1930–1973), a man who oversaw the dramatic growth and development of the city. In his front yard stands a remnant from the history of Snider Plaza, an old street lamp. The Daniel family was the first owner of the Snider Plaza land.

In 1984 the city fathers decided to put in modern lighting for the Plaza and the old lamps were to be thrown away. When Kirven heard this he borrowed a truck and rescued one of the lamps. He had to cut it off to fit it under his old hackberry tree, then put it back together, saving the historic lamp for all to see. (See the Snider Plaza Walk for more about its history.)

The land where you are walking now was shown on a 1900 map of Dallas County as the W. L. Daniel Dairy Farm (see the frontispiece of this book).

Turn right and walk south on Dublin, then turn right on Rosedale and walk west to Durham. As you can see, this is a neighborhood in transition. In the early days of SMU, housing developed to the west of the campus. Before 1930 there were only a few scattered homes on the east side of the campus. During the thirties expansion toward the east was so rapid that by World War II the area was checkerboarded with homes. Built during the Depression, these homes are not extravagant but modest. Many have become rent houses or are being torn down to make way for the new houses and apartments you see.

Turn right on Durham, turn left into the alley in the middle of the block between Rosedale and Milton, and follow the alley back to Airline. There's a reason to go alley-hopping here. As you approach the back of the cemetery, you'll see a curve in the alley. In the early thirties roads and alleys were built using mules. In building this alley a sharp left angle would have been required to preserve the land dedicated to Daniel Cemetery, but sharp angles were extremely difficult to make with mules, and difficult for garbage vehicles to navigate. City engineer Kirven requested that the Daniel family allow him to cut a corner off of the cemetery, to which they agreed. As he promised, that corner has not been developed but is still there, just outside the cemetery, with several of the ancient bois d'arc trees Mrs. Daniel planted still standing. The alley then curves back on its way to Airline.

As we pause here to get a better view of some of the gravestones, or to watch the grackles perform their mating dance on this hallowed ground, the familiar words of Gray's "Elegy" come to mind again:

> *The boast of heraldry, the pomp of pow'r,*
> *And all that beauty, all that wealth e'er gave,*
> *Awaits alike th'inevitable hour.*
> *The paths of glory lead but to the grave.*

In 1896 one of Mrs. Daniel's granddaughters deeded this acreage to the heirs and descendants of the Daniel family, who are today the only ones who can be buried here. The city maintains the outside of the cemetery, and the family takes care of the inside grounds.

The name Daniel conjures up many images. When the well dried up near the orchard, two Daniel sisters moved over to their land they called "The Thicket," near where Curtis Park is today. They eventually sold the land that became Snider Plaza, and that sale provided for them in their old age. These were the same sisters who bought their groceries near where Culwell's is today. (See the McFarlin Walk.) On the corner by Culwell's is Daniel Cleaners, owned by Daniel descendants. The original street signs in University Park misspelled the street named for the family "Daniels." Jack Kirven replaced some of these with "Daniel" signs. If you look you may still find some of the old signs.

While most of the original Daniel 640-acre section has been sold off, Daniel Cemetery remains as tangible evidence of the very first residents of University Park. The buffalo prairie they purchased has blossomed and flourished into a peaceful, tree-lined residential and academic community.

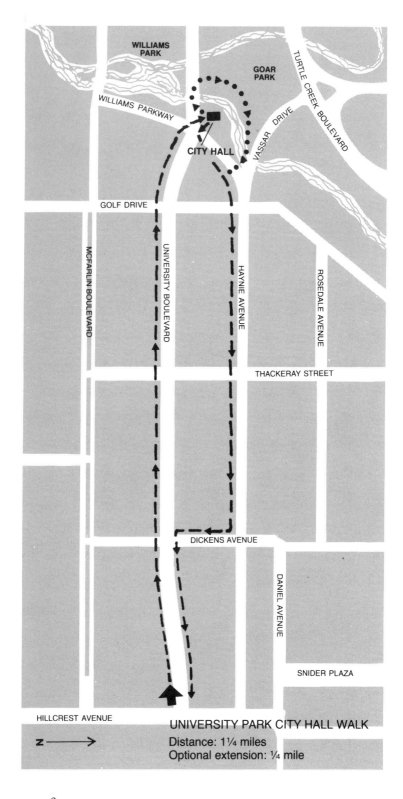

WILLIAMS PARK

GOAR PARK

TURTLE CREEK BOULEVARD

WILLIAMS PARKWAY

VASSAR DRIVE

CITY HALL

GOLF DRIVE

MCFARLIN BOULEVARD

UNIVERSITY BOULEVARD

HAYNIE AVENUE

ROSEDALE AVENUE

THACKERAY STREET

DICKENS AVENUE

DANIEL AVENUE

SNIDER PLAZA

HILLCREST AVENUE

N ⟶

UNIVERSITY PARK CITY HALL WALK

Distance: 1¼ miles
Optional extension: ¼ mile

University Park City Hall Walk

*It is a crying shame that property owners cannot be com-
pelled by law to build sidewalks in front of their premises
and to keep the sidewalks in repair . . . well paved streets
and cement sidewalks not only make a city but enhance
property values and make life worth the living. Every man
should be willing to shoulder his share of the cost. The revenues of the city are large but not large enough to justify the
expectations that residence streets will ever be bricked or
asphalted at the cost of tax payers.*
—Beau Monde magazine, December 6, 1902

$\mathbf{A}$S MOTHERS push their babies in canopied
strollers, with tots tricycling behind them, and ear-
phoned fitness walkers stride briskly along, it's doubt-
ful they stop to think about what it would be like in
University Park without its sidewalks. Look around
you as you stroll along University Boulevard, the first
paved street in University Park, and enjoy going
where its sidewalks take you. Goar Park, for instance,
is always the center of activity, surrounded by rippling
brooks and rolling green grasslands and crowned with
its white gazebo, like a queen watching over her tiny
soccer-playing subjects. The sidewalk trickles through
the park like a brook itself, winding along the creek
and around the playing fields, inviting walkers, bik-
ers, and joggers to enter and partake of its shade and
serenity.

Beau Monde's editors were right—sidewalks, if not
exactly making "life worth the living," do indeed enhance the neighborhood.

University Park City Hall Walk

BEGIN your walk at the corner of University and Hillcrest and walk west on University. Of all the streets in University Park, University Boulevard near Hillcrest probably looks more like it did in the early days than any other street. University Boulevard was the first paved road in University Park, and many of the original homes are still standing, among the oldest in University Park. They were built by a most professional group of first homeowners.

When Southern Methodist University opened in 1915, the new professors needed homes, and Dallas was so far away that they chose to build west of the campus. There were already a few homes in the area, but with the opening of SMU the expansion was rapid. Many of SMU's early faculty lived in "garage houses" while their "big houses" were being built.

When the families of these distinguished professors and ministers needed dental care, they needed only to seek out their neighbor at 3411 University, Dr. S. L. Boren, a dentist who built his home in 1919. The house at 3415 University was owned by Prof. Kilgore, who was acting president of SMU between the terms of Boaz and Selecman. At 3417 is a house built by Dr. Schuessler of SMU that has since served as a parsonage for the Methodist Church, the home of SMU's fourth president, Dr. Umphrey Lee, and later as a boardinghouse for SMU students after World War II. Around 1915 the man who founded the education department at SMU, Dr. Nichols, built the house at 3425, which still retains the original nickel-plated brass hardware, delicate leaded glass front door, and Rookwood fireplace.

From the beginning a neighborly spirit has prevailed on this shaded street, with lots of swapping of eggs and conversation over back fences. Dr. Claude Albritton, Jr., whose father built their home at 3436 University in 1936, represents the only remaining original family. He can describe in glowing terms not only all his present neighbors, but most of the former homeowners as well. At their annual street party the neighbors like to swap favorite raccoon stories and tales about weird pet animals that have appeared here.

This is University Boulevard looking east in about 1915. In the distance is SMU's Dallas Hall. *Courtesy of the SMU Archives*

A publication advertising University Park in 1915 showed this map and stated that "University Boulevard begins at Dallas Hall and curves gracefully westward to Preston Road, which is one of the main pike roads into Dallas. The parked avenue, Bishop Boulevard [now McFarlin], running west from Dallas Hall, will connect directly with Turtle Creek Boulevard, which, when completed, will be one of the most beautiful scenic driveways in the Southwest. Note the streetcar line running from University by Powell's Training School to the city [Dallas, of course]." *Courtesy of the SMU Archives*

3444 University

Perhaps the most magnificent house in the neighborhood is the one at 3444 University, once known as "Mouzon's Folly." It was built around 1915 by the first dean of theology at SMU, Bishop E. DuBose Mouzon, one of the men who persuaded the Methodist church to locate a university in Dallas. The Greek Revival–style exterior has not been changed substantially. The house has five coal-grate fireplaces, probably the only source of heat when it was built. It has been used for a Kappa Alpha Theta sorority house, Kappa Alpha fraternity house, boardinghouse, and apartment house, and is now owned by the Marvin Wise family. The home received historic designation from the Park Cities Historical Society in 1988.

SMU's first president, Robert S. Hyer, built a home not far from here, near the intersection of what is now Daniel and Hillcrest, and maintained a little dairy pasture near where the donut shop on Hillcrest is today. Bishop Mouzon's enterprising son Edwin would walk up to the dairy each morning to get milk, then peddle it door to door up and down the street. Edwin later became a distinguished professor of math at SMU and eventually the chairman of the Southwest Athletic Conference.

A neighbor at 3528 University was a Methodist minister, Dr. Horace Bishop, who was one of the first to sign the cor-

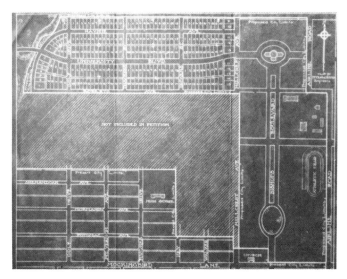

This Myers and Noyes plat of University Park shows the area the city fathers petitioned to incorporate in 1924. Notice the proposed city limits, which include only the SMU campus and homes on three streets. *Courtesy of the SMU Archives*

nerstone at SMU. Bishop Boulevard on the SMU campus was named for him. He built his Prairie-style home around 1915, making it one of the oldest. In fact, by the time University Park was incorporated in 1924, most of the homes you are walking past along University had already been built. Many have been updated but still retain the original styles. Mrs. Margaret Hyer Thomas, daughter of SMU's first president, once lived at 3630 University, built in 1931.

SMU provided the water and sewer for these early homes, but it soon became clear that they could not continue to provide these services for such a mushrooming community. The homeowners tried to annex themselves to Highland Park, which had its hands full providing for its own expansion. The City of Dallas had no interest in joining with such a distant community, a decision they would later regret greatly. Why should Dallas bother to extend its utilities to a small community sitting out in the country with little beyond but Oklahoma? Some of the leaders of this new little community decided to incorporate to furnish water, sewer, garbage removal, and police and fire protection. When they incorporated in April, 1924, more than 380 homes had already been built. One of the men who helped incorporate the city, W. P. Clements, didn't know that his son Bill would someday become governor of Texas.

While Highland Park was touted from the beginning as an exclusive residential community, University Park advertised its community as a cultural and intellectual center being carved out of university land. For many years the city limit signs read, "University Park—Home of SMU, Many Churches, and Excellent Schools." Yet Highland Park built a library in 1930, while late in the eighties, University Park was still the largest city in Texas without its own library. For many years University Park residents were allowed to use the small Highland Park Library as well as SMU's library. But in the 1970s nonresident fees began in Highland Park, and University Park residents no longer can check out books from SMU due to its burgeoning student population, increasing University Park's need for a community library.

Cross Golf Drive and continue on University as it curves toward the park. You'll begin to see the City Hall, which is not the original building erected in 1924. The original building was a plain two-story structure, and while it was being built the city fathers met in Dallas Hall at SMU. In 1937 the City Hall was rebuilt and expanded for $65,000. The architect, Grayson Gill, was sent to Williamsburg, Virginia, to study its architecture. When he returned the City Hall was given this distinctly American style, a faithful but smaller reproduction of the Governor's Palace in Williamsburg. The brickwork was completely redone with special sand-molded brick brought in from Mineral Wells, Texas. The original 1924 cornerstone was then put back where you see it now, near the front door. The simplicity of the exterior makes it dependent on this brickwork for its character. The roof covering is clay shingle tile, the same as that used on early Virginia buildings. On top is a copper-plated tower that is regularly polished to keep it gleaming in the sun. In 1937 the fire department wing was added behind the main building in an unobtrusive, set-back style with the same special brick.

Step inside the main door of the City Hall to see some traditional Williamsburg touches that were retained when the building was further remodeled and enlarged in 1973. The colonial stairway remains, as do the paneled wainscots, now painted over, and the denticulated cornices, all of wood. Although the interior lighting is modern, it ties in with the Georgian theme. On the walls are various bronze commemorative plaques. Halfway up the stairs a bronze

University Park City Hall is shown in 1948 with an addition on the right for the police department. During World War II an air raid siren was installed on the north side of the cupola. *Courtesy of Jack Kirven*

plaque shows the original City Hall in 1924, before taking on the Williamsburg style. Directly above the main floor is the council chamber, also used as the municipal court-room. It is one and one-half stories high, lighted in part by the second-story and dormer windows, with exposed trusses set in Texas gum wood, and wood-paneled wain-scots. The various city offices are down the hallways.

Stepping back outside, notice the north wing of the building, added in 1973. The work was so well done and the brick so perfectly matched that it is nearly impossible to tell which section was done in 1937 (the main building and fire station wing) and which in 1973 (the north wing).

Underneath the north wing and the parking lot beside it, the remains of an artesian well drilled in 1915 at the request of SMU lie buried. It was drilled to a depth of 2,850 feet into the Trinity Sands, and on top a small pump station with several large air compressors was built. There were two circular cooling towers, yet when water was pumped to the new SMU Dallas Hall, it was 106 to 108 degrees, so hot there was no need for water-heating equipment in the building. Early residents used to drive to the well and bring home jugs of water, driving home slowly to allow them time to cool.

Another well was drilled for the city later at the southeast corner of Stanford and Thackeray, and in 1925 a third well was drilled for SMU at Airline and McFarlin near their steam plant, to a depth of 2,999 feet. These three artesian wells served the community until 1934 when the city had to start purchasing water from Dallas on a wholesale basis. The city then began talking about forming a water district with Highland Park. The artesian wells were eventually capped, and in 1947 a water district was created for the Park Cities.

If you could use Superman's X-ray vision, you could see under the pavement on University Boulevard the large pipes carrying water from Lake Grapevine, the cleanest water in the Dallas area. The water is treated in the Park Cities water plant on Harry Hines, then routed to an underground booster pump near Germany Park (Lomo Alto and the Tollway). The booster pump sends the water down University to two storage tanks. The first one was built near SMU next to the Daniel Cemetery and holds half a million gallons. Later a 2.5-million-gallon tank was added at Coffee Park (Villanova at Hillcrest). These tanks now deliver water into University Park homes upon demand. The tank near Daniel Cemetery will soon be replaced with a larger one.

The park adjacent to the City Hall is Goar Park, named in 1947—the same year the water district was created—for a former University Park judge and city attorney. Goar Park is the site of weekly soccer and football games and family picnics, and the destination of the annual Park Cities Fourth of July parade. The parade began in 1963 as a Jaycee civic and fund-raising project. Hundreds of citizens, many arriving on crepe-paper-strewn floats and bicycles, trucks and even tanks, in strollers, on skates, and on foot, gather to celebrate their country's independence. There are lemonade stands for refreshment, and a Dixieland band

and sometimes a military band for entertainment. The mayor and other local citizens make patriotic speeches from the gazebo before announcing winners of the bicycle decorating contest. The afternoon continues as did turn-of-the-century July Fourth celebrations, with picnicking on the grounds and games and sack races for kids of all ages. The residents of many blocks get together the night before to decorate a float for the parade—the redder, whiter, and bluer the better!

Long before Goar Park became the site of the city's official July Fourth celebration, it was the first location of the Park Cities YMCA. The original building was the home of Judge J. N. Townsend at 3802 University, located near where the gazebo stands today. The house and land were purchased by Highland Park, University Park, and the YMCA. In 1946 Townsend's home was remodeled to accommodate the growing "Y" program. In 1951 the YMCA moved to its present location on Preston Road.

If you wish to get a better view of the park and gazebo, take a short side trip by crossing the creek on University and turning right into the park. (If not, continue past City Hall to Haynie for your return trip.) The new gazebo is the achievement of the University Park Foundation, led by University Park residents Peter and Frances Chantillis. The July Fourth celebration had outgrown the decorated flatbed of a trailer truck used as a bandstand and speakers' podium. The Foundation began to raise funds from private sources to build a gazebo to serve this function, one big enough to hold a symphony orchestra. As the bronze plaque on the northeast corner tells, the gazebo was proudly dedicated on July 4, 1980. The names of all the donors can be found on a bronze plaque in the City Hall, near the downstairs elevator.

Cross the creek at Vassar Drive to get to Haynie, and continue east on Haynie for your return trip. The first three paved streets in University Park were University, Haynie, and McFarlin. It was not unusual during those first years to be awakened by a rooster's morning call, for people still kept cows, ponies, ducks, and chickens in their backyards. The land immediately north was still undeveloped farmland. Not until 1939 did the city ban the keeping of farm animals.

While there are many newer buildings mixed in with

The house on the southwest corner of Haynie and Golf, bull-dozed in the mid-eighties, was for many years the oldest structure in University Park, perhaps dating back as early as 1907. *Courtesy of the Town of Highland Park*

older structures on Haynie, a careful inspection of the early homes sprinkled with a touch of imagination will re-create the flavor of the neighborhood in its fledgling days. A scattering of Prairie-style homes, Tudor cottages, quaint bungalows, and early Georgian homes remain, dating back to the days before incorporation when SMU provided all their city services. Most of the homes have been nicely up-dated in the original styles.

Be sure to notice the house at 3500 Haynie, built between 1913 and 1915. It is called the Mourning House because its owner, a widow, lost both her husband and her son within six months of each other. She had the house painted black to signify her state of mourning. Later owners retained its color, and only in recent years has it been repainted in its present olive green shade.

Turn right on Dickens and left on University to return to your starting point. University Park has nothing to mourn today. The community can boast eight churches, including the largest congregation of any Presbyterian church in the United States, Highland Park Presbyterian Church, and one of the largest congregations of any Methodist church in the United States, Highland Park United Methodist Church. University Park provides over forty acres of parkland and over a hundred miles of sidewalks, one of the finest universities in the Southwest, one of the most outstanding school systems in the country, and perhaps someday it will have its own library.

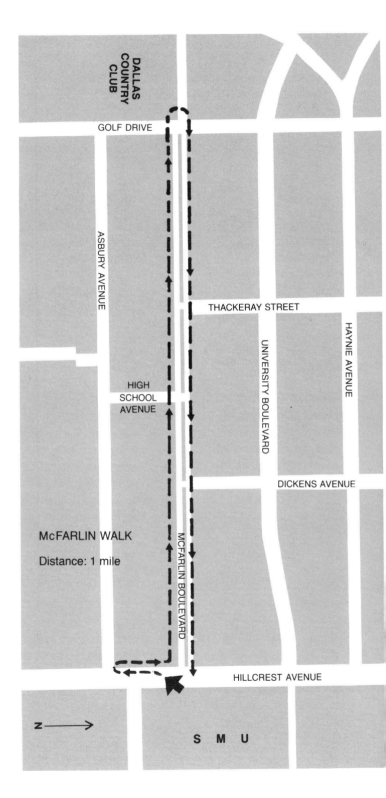

DALLAS COUNTRY CLUB

GOLF DRIVE

ASBURY AVENUE

THACKERAY STREET

HAYNIE AVENUE

UNIVERSITY BOULEVARD

HIGH SCHOOL AVENUE

DICKENS AVENUE

McFARLIN WALK

Distance: 1 mile

McFARLIN BOULEVARD

HILLCREST AVENUE

N →

S M U

McFarlin Walk

MYTHOLOGY was the Greeks' way of explaining the world around them. It was early science as well as early literature. The Greeks made their gods in their own images, with weaknesses as well as strengths. Zeus, for example, was perpetually trying to hide his love affairs from Hera, his jealous wife, who was always ingeniously trying to trip him up. Yet Greek artists and poets also realized how strong, straight, and swift man could really be. Homer's *Odyssey* speaks of "the divine for which all men long." Thus the thunder and lightning was transformed into the universal father, Zeus, the savior and guardian of mankind.

As human beings we seem to need ideals to strive for and people of vision to carry them out for us. History is filled with accounts of dreamers and visionaries whose ideas achieved, or sometimes failed to achieve, reality.

Studying the history of the Park Cities, one begins to realize a subtle difference between the two communities. Like the beautiful Athena, Zeus's favorite daughter who sprang full-blown from his head, Highland Park seemed to spring full-blown from the grand ideas of developers Henry Exall and John Armstrong. Educated and traveled businessmen, they had the foresight to plan a unified, exclusive parkland community with ideas drawn from such diverse places as Philadelphia, Beverly Hills, and Barcelona, Spain. Sometimes they felt hard ideas were necessary, such as having no church buildings in the community. Bold tactics were used, such as the luring of an established country club into their midst. Strict building codes were hammered out and enforced from the beginning. These steps were carried out by Armstrong's sons-in-law, Edgar Flippen and Hugh Prather, who, unlike Eurydice leading Orpheus out of Hades, never looked back, so sure were they of their goal.

On the other hand, University Park has grown up somewhat like Highland Park's little brother, wet behind the ears, its development uneven and scattered. Its leaders were salt-of-the-earth pioneers who came here to farm, raise cattle, establish businesses and even a university, teach, and provide for their families. There was perhaps more equality here, more democracy, less exclusiveness than in Highland Park.

One early leader with great vision, Dr. Robert S. Hyer, spent many of his productive years on the creation of Southern Methodist University, which despite some difficult times has developed into one of the outstanding universities in the Southwest. But much of University Park beyond the SMU campus, like Topsy in *Uncle Tom's Cabin*, just "growed." Only late in the development of the community have the city fathers begun to look at the facts and place more stringent requirements on builders and developers. Not until 1940 was a strict zoning ordinance established. Nearly too late University Park realized that Dallas had grown around them and gobbled up the tax bases such as Preston Center West that would have helped to stabilize University Park's financial position. Over one-third of all property in University Park is non-taxable, and a widened Central Expressway will take another sizable chunk away from the city's taxable property.

Perhaps University Park is finally coming of age and realizing it has yet to achieve its true greatness, to tie the community more closely together with the strong sense of vision and civic pride that Highland Park seems to have been born with. University Park is beginning to ask hard questions and find answers for them. Little brother is growing up.

McFarlin Walk

BEGIN your walk at the corner of McFarlin and Hill-crest, on the south side of McFarlin. As you look across Hillcrest to the SMU campus, try to imagine a field of Johnson grass without a single tree, and only a few impos-ing buildings emerging from the bald prairie. Imagine on the corner behind you just one red brick building housing University Grocery, a barber shop, and Couches' Drug Store, with a metal shack attached where Wendell E. Cul-well started a pressing business in 1919. (Later Hillcrest State Bank would be added in the building.) Look to the north and imagine the two Daniel sisters, Fannie and Georgia, granddaughters of Frances Sims Daniel, sporting their bonnets and walking across the fields past a few scat-tered houses to buy their groceries.

Some say that this was the area's only food store from its opening in 1922 until grocery chains appeared in about 1939, while others claim they remember a small grocery near the theater in Snider Plaza around 1930. The Univer-sity Grocery bought milk from Mowatt's Dairy, southeast of the SMU campus where a shopping center now stands.

Walk south on Hillcrest toward Asbury. In 1920 when space became available in the front part of the red brick building, Culwell moved there and added cleaning and tai-loring to his business. The bronze plaque by today's front door and the sign above the door both are dated 1920. Until then residents had to go all the way to Knox Street, near where the Katy Railroad Station would be built in 1922, to have a suit made or cleaned. W. E. Culwell's boiler leaked something awful in his small shop, and times were lean for a while. Ladies began asking his tailor to sell them some thread, and by 1926 the Varsity Cleaners had become the Varsity Shop. By 1928 it had added the first delivery truck. Business was slow again during the Depression, although Dallas was not hit as hard as other places because it had become a pivotal point of the Southwest's immense oil business with the discovery of the East Texas oil field. But the Varsity Shop would have to survive two fires before be-coming Culwell and Son in 1976.

On the corner of Hillcrest and Asbury where Daniel Cleaners is located today stood Turner's Mustang Phar-macy with its popular soda fountain, perhaps so popular

In February 1926 this photo was taken looking southwest to Hill-crest between McFarlin and Asbury from the top of McFarlin Auditorium. The two-story building housed University Grocery, a barber shop, a drugstore, and Culwell's Varsity Cleaners. On the left near Asbury is Fox's Garage, and east of Hillcrest are the trolley tracks. *Courtesy of the SMU Archives*

The Mustang Pharmacy, located on the "Drag" on Hillcrest between McFarlin and Asbury, had a soda fountain that was popular with SMU students. *Courtesy of the SMU Archives*

because the store was cooled by the first central air condi-
tioning unit in Dallas. The old compressor is still sitting in
the back of Daniel Cleaners, too heavy to move. The Pharmacy served tall frozen malts for five cents and T-bone
steak dinners for fifty-five cents. Nearby was Shorty Wilson's, a coffee shop, described by one former student as
"the heart and soul of SMU off campus." Here you might
find impromptu pep rallies or captured Aggies having their
heads shaved.

Walk back north toward McFarlin. Between Daniel
Cleaners and the Varsity Shop was Fox's Garage and Service Station. Notice the hump in the pavement all the way
across the parking area covering the place where the old
gas tanks were located. This whole block was referred to
by students as "The Drag." The Daniel family started its
cleaning business in 1925 in a small building on Asbury behind the present store, selling men's slacks and ties as well.
By the time Daniel Cleaners moved to the present location
in 1958, there were five cleaners in the neighborhood. And
if any of the businesses needed ice, they only had to walk
across Asbury Street to the ice house.

As the hum of constant traffic and the blare of horns
brings you back to the present day, **turn left and walk west
on the south side of McFarlin.** Begin looking for some of the
early houses. For some reason housing started and spread
west of SMU, not east. McFarlin was one of only three
paved streets when SMU opened in 1915. It's so bumpy because it was originally paved by wheelbarrow loads.

McFarlin Boulevard was first called Roberts Boulevard in
honor of Mrs. Dora Roberts of Big Spring, Texas, who gave
one of the three largest original founding gifts to SMU in
1913. But by the late 1920s the third president of SMU had
forgotten about her and changed the name to McFarlin
Boulevard in honor of the R. M. McFarlins of San Antonio,
who donated nearly $500,000 to build a new auditorium.
The renaming proved to be a costly mistake. Understand-
ably upset, Mrs. Roberts withdrew $100,000 slated to go to
SMU and gave it to Southwestern University at Georgetown instead.

Originally the south side of McFarlin was not paved. The
islands in the middle were at that time a high embankment
covered with bois d'arc trees all the way down "Roberts
Boulevard." When University Park incorporated in 1924,
the area on the south side of the street asked to be in-

cluded, and the embankment was then cut down along with the trees to form the boulevard you see today.

While some of the oldest homes in University Park are clustered on McFarlin Boulevard, demolition and new construction have occurred fairly extensively in University Park—more so than in Highland Park. Few blocks are without intrusive, large-scale new structures, although some of the new homes are tastefully done. New duplexes as well as brick duplexes from the twenties and thirties are scattered among the remaining frame bungalows and Prairie-style homes built during SMU's early development.

The size of the trees on some lots betrays the age of the homes. The nubby trunk and spreading branches of an antique magnolia tree waft sweet smells in the summer over the house at 3521 McFarlin, which has been converted to a duplex. Be sure to notice a Prairie-style home flanked by two old trees at 3601 McFarlin, built in 1914 or 1915, called the McKinley House. It's a little frame house built with very narrow boards, which indicate its age. Nearby at 3613 look for a chimney that bears a bas-relief masonry picture of a sailing ship. Often these early developer houses show an English influence, with small stained glass or leaded glass windows, brick arched openings, and steep roofs.

At Golf Drive by the northern part of Dallas Country Club, cross over to the north side of McFarlin and return east. Look up as you pass under the tall sycamore tree rustling in the wind. All the way along McFarlin stand towering trees that have provided successive generations with welcome shade on a summer day.

By 1939 University Park had rapidly expanded north of Lovers Lane, filling what was once farmland, and the McFarlin area had become "Old University Park." Dallas had begun to have a real interest in this beautiful residential community growing up by SMU and touted as a cultural and intellectual center, and was beginning to regret not agreeing to annexation in the early twenties.

In 1939 W. W. Caruth, Sr., son of pioneer William Caruth, and Dr. Umphrey Lee, fourth president of SMU, requested that University Park annex a 233-acre portion of their joint estate (Caruth had given one-half interest in over seven hundred acres of land to SMU). This annexation extended the boundaries of University Park to Northwest Highway and Preston Road, forestalling Dallas's plan to include the land in the proposed new township of Preston Hollow.

By the war year of 1945 University Park had a population of over twenty thousand, and Dallas was still pressing University Park for a vote on annexation. After much heated discussion, the question was brought to a vote, eliciting a large turnout considering that many voters were away serving their country. But the citizens of University Park turned Dallas down by a vote of 2,017 to 1,726. The next day Dallas annexed everything around University Park.

Other interesting elections took place around this time, too. During the fifties there must have been little to argue about, because the big topic of discussion was whether or not to restrain dogs. This great issue split the community wide open, even breaking up some longtime business partnerships. The commissioners decided taking a vote was safer than taking a stand, so the ballots were cast. In a hotly contested race, 1,950 citizens voted to require leashes, while 1,910 voted against it. In a mayor's race a few weeks later, only 56 voters showed up to elect their new leader.

As you continue walking east to Hillcrest under the shade trees in this peaceful neighborhood, it's apparent that the first residents of this university town were not a wealthy crowd. But they lived in comfort a stone's throw from the campus where many of them worked by day, near the families they were raising. With a little effort one can almost imagine the sounds of the professors' children laughing and playing long ago in the shade of the trees amidst the hypnotic hum of katydids on a lazy summer afternoon. Or are those today's children one hears?

The children of SMU's first football coach, Ray Morrison, played near their white house at 3540 McFarlin. Today's children swing from the same tree, grown much taller, that was in the Morrisons' front yard.

During the forties the City of University Park continued to expand its boundaries when it annexed all of the area between University Boulevard and Mockingbird Lane as far east as Greenville Avenue, the section including the old Cowboy Building and the old Dr Pepper plant. Thirty days later they gave up this gold mine of a tax base and de-annexed it because some of the citizens didn't want "all those beer joints" in University Park. Did University Park's leaders, like Eurydice, make a mistake by looking

By the 1940s Dallas decided it wanted to consolidate with University Park, as shown in this cartoon by John Knott, but the citizens of University Park turned down Dallas's proposal of "marriage." *Courtesy of the Dallas Morning News*

back and changing their minds? Or did they try to preserve the quiet and peaceful homelife, such as was found along McFarlin, only later to realize that this might also be their Achilles' heel?

University Park has come a long way since its beginnings near the SMU campus. Its boundaries have expanded and issues concerning various aspects of its growth have been resolved. The decisions to be made by a growing city are complex. Taking a stand on important issues is not always easy or popular. Hopefully University Park's present and future leaders will prove to be men and women with vision as well as civic pride, able to take hard stands—leaders whose ideas will achieve reality.

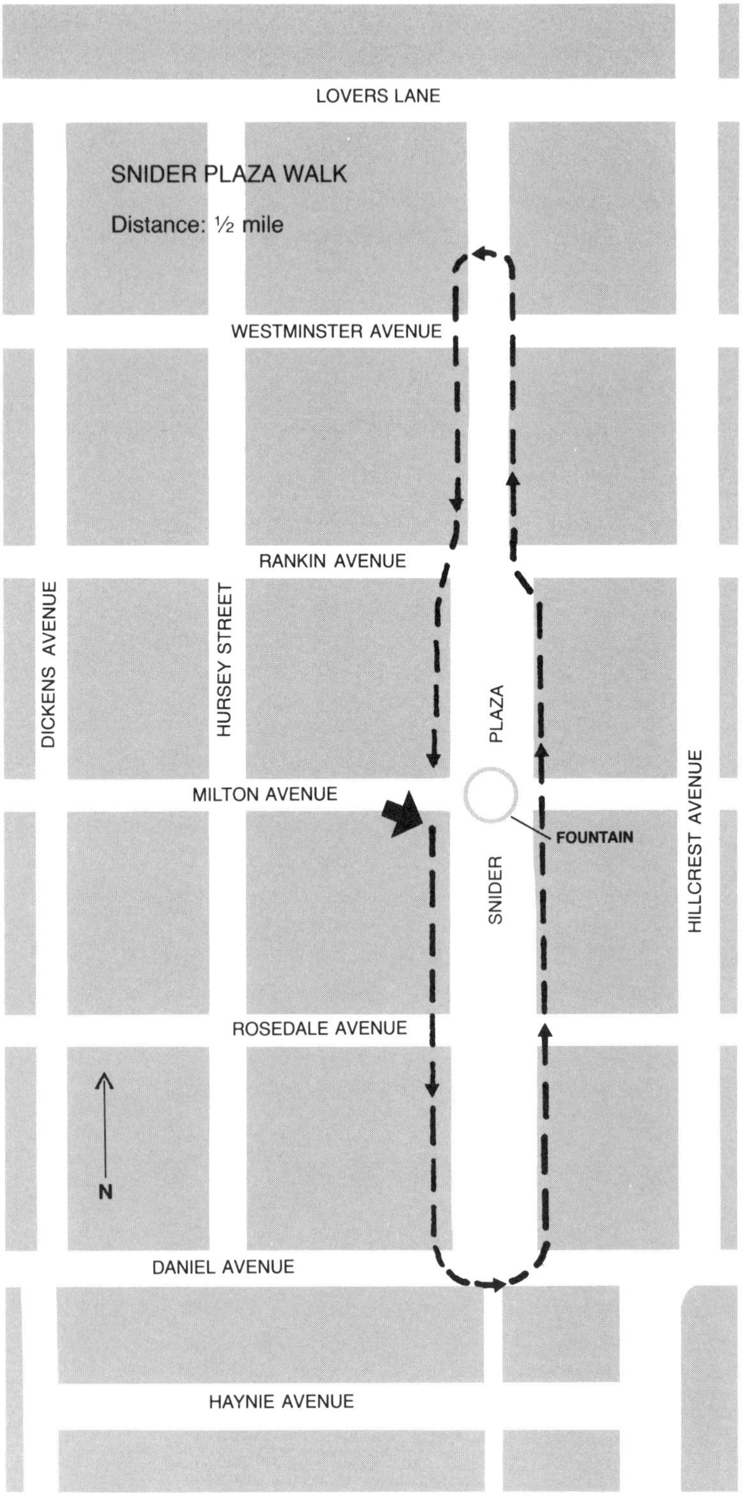

SNIDER PLAZA WALK

Distance: ½ mile

LOVERS LANE

WESTMINSTER AVENUE

RANKIN AVENUE

DICKENS AVENUE

HURSEY STREET

MILTON AVENUE

PLAZA

SNIDER

FOUNTAIN

HILLCREST AVENUE

ROSEDALE AVENUE

N

DANIEL AVENUE

HAYNIE AVENUE

180

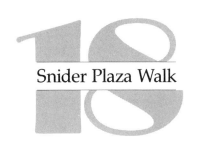

Snider Plaza Walk

THERE'S A certain curiosity in each of us that gets us up out of our chairs and sends us off in search of the new, the unusual. Long vacations to faraway places are not uncommon for many families in our jet age. Trips to the moon and beyond are not outside the realm of possibility for future generations.

But no matter where we travel, too often we are struck by how much the same the world is becoming, with chain hotels and stores, franchise restaurants, tall buildings, sprawling freeways, and the omnipresent car. Perhaps in our hungry search for the new and different, we have overlooked the beauty and individuality of the place in which we live. For no matter how pleasurable a trip is, there's nothing better than coming home.

Throughout history, a village has been a cluster of homes with whatever establishments were needed to take care of the necessities of life, all within distances accessible on foot. With the advent of gas-guzzling autos, suburbs sprang up based on the assumption that everyone had a car. Homes were far from shopping, nothing was within walking distance, and some suburbs were built with no sidewalks at all.

Even though University Park is located in the middle of one of the largest cities in the United States, it has a down-home, village-type atmosphere. Places of interest are only a few minutes' walk from residents' homes. The temperate climate in Dallas, with over three hundred days per year of sunshine, affords suitable weather to get us up out of our chairs to walk year-round. And don't forget that in University Park alone there are over a hundred miles of sidewalk to walk upon.

Snider Plaza Walk

IT WAS WITH the feeling of a small village that Snider Plaza was founded. C. W. Snider had no desire to establish a shopping center all by himself in one architectural style, such as the Highland Park Village would later become, with its resulting exclusive atmosphere. He wanted each different owner to lend his own style to the place, to create a friendly, down-home spot where neighbors could gather.

Begin your walk at Milton Avenue by the Snider Plaza fountain and the nearby theater. In 1926 Snider came to visit his daughter at Southern Methodist University and to see the groundbreaking ceremony for Snider Hall, a new women's dorm he had just donated $150,000 to build. On that visit he first became interested in developing a business center in this rapidly expanding community. He and J. Fred Smith, the first mayor of University Park (1924–1928), bought eighty acres of prairie for a thousand dollars an acre from the Daniels, land that had been part of the first section the Daniel family bought in 1849. This shopping area would be important in the development of University Park, for until this time most of the closest retail was on Knox Street. The first stores in Highland Park Village would not open until 1931.

Only dirt roads led to the area when paving began in 1927. Lights were installed, and the central fountain you see in front of you was built. The fountain was a big attraction, with many colors of lights and water shooting high into the air. People with cars would drive here at night just to watch it. One rainy night when the pavement was wet and shiny, a flock of Canadian geese flew overhead. Thinking this area was a lake, they tried to land, causing many injuries to the flock. Speaking of wildlife, buffalo used to roam this area to feast on the tall prairie grass. But by 1889 there were only about 550 bison left.

The main attraction of Snider Plaza was to be a $30,000 modern theater showing "talkies," the latest thing in moving pictures. The Varsity Theatre opened in 1929, complete with a Venetian garden setting and a "cry room" for mothers with small children to sit in. On Saturdays the neighborhood kids would all meet their friends at the movies, and a special treat it was during those Depression days.

Adjoining the theater to the north were several other businesses.

The theater caused a stir several years ago. Renamed the Fine Arts Theatre, it began showing X-rated movies, much to the outrage of the community. When the lease expired it was taken over by the Plaza Theatre, which has become a showcase for Broadway and off-Broadway productions.

Begin walking south from the theater. Across the street at the corner of Rosedale you can see where the very first business sprang up in 1927, the Ralph Porter real estate agency. It began as a one-room Williamsburg-style office from which all of the Snider Plaza property was handled. When the office was recently remodeled they went back to the Williamsburg style, on the same corner where the building had originally been located. (It was their dream that someday all the buildings in Snider Plaza would conform to that same style, perhaps drawing in more people, and surely bringing in more tax revenues for University Park.)

Aside from these early buildings, nothing much was added for ten years or so due to the stifling effect of the Depression. Only filling stations were there, because oil companies had the money. Then three more stores were added to the south of the theater. Among these was the Capitol Grill, which became the Highland Park High School hangout, their jukebox blaring into the wee hours, especially on football game nights. None of these stores remains.

South of Rosedale you'll find Pat's Park Cities delicatessen, formerly located at Highland Park Village, sporting historic Park Cities photographs on its interior walls if you care to step inside to view them.

On the corner at Daniel is one of the most popular stores, Kuby's Sausage House, opened in 1961. Kuby brought his father's business from Germany, where it had been in the family for over two hundred years. If you can't get away to Europe, you'll find some grocery items and even foreign magazines from various European countries inside. Don't be surprised to hear many patrons speaking German.

The Hillcrest State Bank, now the Texas Commerce Bank, which you can see across Daniel, achieved fame in 1938 for opening the first drive-in bank in the world. The architect was George Dahl, who was also responsible for directing the construction of the buildings for the 1936 Centennial Exposition at Fair Park, work which played a major part in pulling Dallas out of the Depression. The year of the Centennial, Dahl became president of the Highland Park Independent School District school board.

Across Daniel from the bank (around the corner from the east side of Snider Plaza) is Jerry's Country Smokehouse. It was known for many years as the Beef Bar (later Peggy's Beef Bar), which opened just after World War II and had the distinction, according to *D Magazine*, of serving some of the best onion rings in Dallas.

Return north on the east side of Snider Plaza. As you cross Rosedale, look to your right over to the corner of Hillcrest where you'll see Bubba's restaurant, providing with their fried chicken more of the down-home flavor that Snider envisioned.

The many shops to the north of Ralph Porter's real estate office are located where a miniature golf course once stood. In the next block, across Milton, M. E. Moses is a landmark that has tripled in size since its inception in 1941, being remodeled several times. It's a family operation whose motto is that no sale is complete until the customer is absolutely satisfied. Next door is the Revco (formerly Skillern's) drug store. But before that it was Cleveland's Drug Store where friends could meet at the old soda fountain.

Continue north across Rankin, past the Texaco service station, toward the former Safeway parking lot, now Minyard's, on the corner of Westminster. Try to imagine a bus station here. In the late twenties Ralph Porter started a bus line serving the Park Cities. Six buses ran from Snider Plaza to downtown Dallas for a round trip fare (two tickets) of a quarter; fifty tickets cost five dollars. The Safeway store was built around the same time as M. E. Moses, and the building which you see here, now Minyard's, was completed in 1972. The last major section to be added to Snider Plaza was across the street where the Adele Hunt building is.

Cross to the west side of Snider Plaza and return south to where your walk began, near the fountain. As late as the early fifties, the street would be blocked off and street dances occasionally would be held around the fountain. Eventually Snider gave the fountain to the city to maintain, but it finally went out of use. In 1975 it was reactivated, but people complained because it got their cars wet. The pumping system underground was completely worn out, and in 1987 the tenants and owners in Snider Plaza began raising money to renovate the fountain. With the help of

When Snider Plaza opened in 1927 it contained street lamps, a central fountain (shown in the distance), and one small business, the Ralph Porter Real Estate Agency (seen on the right). *Courtesy of the Dallas Public Library*

Buddy Porter they raised $12,500, and the city contributed $25,000. The restored fountain in front of you was truly a community effort.

In the spring of 1988 a series of University Park Master Plan meetings began at which residents were urged to dream their dreams and try to imagine University Park as they'd like to see it in the year 2010. So before you leave Snider Plaza, imagine for a moment . . . if all the buildings in the Plaza could be revitalized and undergo a unifying face lift, yet keep the down-home flavor . . . if a several-story parking garage were added next to the bank to draw more customers with easier parking . . . would the additional revenues help to bolster the faltering University Park tax base and allow it to have once again the unique distinction of having the lowest tax rate in the county? A dream? Perhaps. But today's dreams are tomorrow's realities.

The restored fountain, a perfect example of what community effort can accomplish, is a step toward that reality. Perhaps in the future the fountain will help draw together teenagers as well as adults for old-fashioned evenings of ice cream and conversation, even occasional street dances like the ones in the "old days." A place where neighbors and friends could gather in a homey, relaxed place was just what C. W. Snider envisioned over sixty years ago.

Now that you know a little bit about the background of Snider Plaza, take time to visit some of the shops that caught your eye. There is a whole row of businesses on Hillcrest as well.

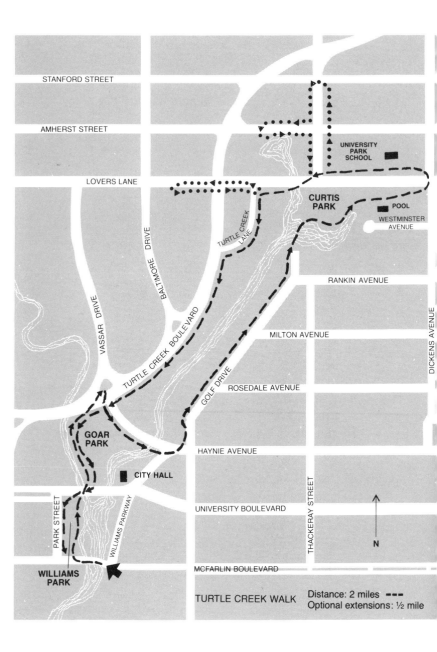

STANFORD STREET

AMHERST STREET

LOVERS LANE

BALTIMORE DRIVE

VASSAR DRIVE

TURTLE CREEK LANE

TURTLE CREEK BOULEVARD

GOLF DRIVE

CURTIS PARK

UNIVERSITY PARK SCHOOL

POOL

WESTMINSTER AVENUE

RANKIN AVENUE

MILTON AVENUE

ROSEDALE AVENUE

DICKENS AVENUE

GOAR PARK

CITY HALL

HAYNIE AVENUE

PARK STREET

WILLIAMS PARKWAY

THACKERAY STREET

UNIVERSITY BOULEVARD

N

WILLIAMS PARK

MCFARLIN BOULEVARD

TURTLE CREEK WALK

Distance: 2 miles ---
Optional extensions: ½ mile

Turtle Creek Walk

TURTLES, like all reptiles, are cold-blooded, which means their body temperature stays about the same as the surrounding water or air. They can't be active in cold weather, so they can't live in regions that are cold throughout the year. Dallas is particularly suited for turtles because of our normally mild winters.

The most spectacular of all reptiles, the dinosaur, also lived in this region. Recently one of the richest early dinosaur sites ever excavated was discovered near Stephenville, and three skeletons were brought to Southern Methodist University. But unlike the dinosaur, which became extinct long ago, the turtle survives today.

Turtle Creek, which runs through the Park Cities, this "creek with all the turtles" as early travelers called it, is the home of many of these creatures whose kind have survived 185 million years. When we see a turtle along this stream, perhaps it will serve as a reminder, not just of the longevity of the turtle, but of the brevity of our own lives, and of human life on this earth.

Turtle Creek Walk

BEGIN your walk on McFarlin Boulevard at the bridge over Turtle Creek, near the intersection of McFarlin and Williams Parkway, one block south of the University Park City Hall. In the same year the City Hall was being built, 1924, the city completely blocked the original channel of Turtle Creek at McFarlin by filling it with earth and putting a paved roadway on top, with a small box culvert underneath. During heavy rains this intersection would be inundated with over two feet of water. In the 1950s the city used the latest of concrete techniques to build a new culvert and spillway by cutting and laying huge half sections of pipe. Jack Kirven, city engineer from 1930 to 1973, remembers cutting one side a little shorter than the other so the pieces would fit the rise in the hill. Take a minute to walk down the stairs at the stone bridge and view the results. Children have even been known to crawl under the road. If water is standing on the lower steps on the north side of the bridge, try the south side.

The house just west of the bridge, at 3805 McFarlin, was built in 1932 for $25,000 for University Park mayor Elbert Williams by the architect David Williams (not related), who designed the Loma Linda walls. (See the Loma Linda Walk.) The house attracted national attention when it was written up in *American Home* magazine in 1935 and *Better Homes and Gardens* in 1937 as a rambling Texas ranch house. It characterizes the architect's indigenous regional style better than any others and was the last private residence he built.

The house contains all the features that Williams considered necessary for comfortable southwestern living, such as light brick to reflect the sun, standing seam copper roof, thick walls, balconies, patios, and shuttered windows. The architect loved Texana, and each house has a decorative motif that is carried throughout. He used his favorite emblem here, the star, symbolic of the Lone Star State of Texas. It appears inside as cutout shapes on the handmade cupboards, cabinets, and even on the dining chairs. (The house is not open to the public.) On the exterior, see if you can find the star, which is used both as cutouts and in three dimensions on wood.

The house at 3819 McFarlin was built by architect Charles

3805 McFarlin

Dilbeck, who claimed that while Williams built city-type Texas houses, he developed ranch-style Texas houses. (For more on Dilbeck see the Loma Linda Walk.)

Take the sidewalk on the west side of the bridge and walk north into the park toward the tennis courts. An aerial map of University Park in 1930 shows that the two tennis courts were already here, the first tennis courts built in the city. As you walk by the lake, try to ignore the styrofoam cups, beer cans, plastic bags, and miscellaneous trash floating by and concentrate on the azaleas or crape myrtles, depending on the season.

In 1972 a $1 million bond issue was passed to make the lakes in University Park more useful and attractive and to improve the water. The problem was complex because the city's storm sewers drained into Turtle Creek and the lakes, filling them with silt. Storm sewers were moved to bypass the lakes, which were then drained and dredged down to the old creek beds. Muck and dirt were removed, and walls were repaired, using broken concrete. As the water returned, some of the waterfowl returned. The Texas Parks and Wildlife Department began a fish management program, providing blue gill, channel catfish fingerlings, and black bass. Out of Turtle Creek was created a chain of "managed urban lakes"—Williams, Curtis, and Caruth—with the creek itself being used as a natural open-space corridor winding through the area around the City Hall.

Williams Park was created in 1939 and named for Elbert Williams while he was serving his term as fourth mayor of University Park (1938–1942). There is a bronze marker just to the north of the lake, under the trees on the little peninsula east of the tennis courts. The imaginative playground with its crabapple trees, west of the tennis courts, was created for children over age five. If you bring a toddler here, keep a close watch. More than one child has been rescued from the top of the giant half circle. After scrambling up, some children realize they don't know how to scramble down. Notice the venerable old cottonwood tree at the north end of the tennis courts.

Cross University and follow the sidewalk along the western branch of the creek, through Goar Park. Chances are good, if the day is sunny, that you'll see one of the holdovers from prehistoric times, the turtle, sunning himself on a log. **When you reach the street (Turtle Creek Boulevard, although you can't see the sign from here), swing to the right and cross over to the triangle called Byrd Parkway where Vassar splits in two.** Before she died, Mattie Caruth Byrd (daughter of W. W. Caruth, Sr., and wife of Harold Byrd) lived just up Vassar Drive. Read the marker at the southwest point of the triangle as well as the one under the statue.

A 1959 aerial photo looking south from Lovers Lane shows Curtis Park. The street angling to the right is Golf Drive, and in the distance is the University Park City Hall. In Goar Park you can see the first YMCA building. *Courtesy of Jack Kirven*

Cross back to Goar Park and walk south on Vassar to the sidewalk that leads to the gazebo. The bronze marker on the northeast corner of the gazebo tells about its dedication in 1980. Nearby is one of several groves of live oak trees growing in the parks dedicated to former mayors.

Continue south on Vassar, cross the bridge, and round the corner to the left to walk north up Golf Drive, past the magnificent homes that share the creek in their backyards with the homes on Turtle Creek Boulevard. While most of the land in University Park in pioneer days was prairie filled with Johnson grass, or cotton fields, trees could be found along the creeks, such as the giant old bois d'arc, hackberry, cottonwood, elm, and a few pecan trees you see. Look up Rosedale and Milton as you pass by to see sprawling bois d'arc trees that have offered summer shade for countless generations. Fortunately the homeowners have had the foresight to save these ancient trees. There is a distinctive orange color of the wood where the bark has fallen away. A yellow dye can be made by boiling chips of the wood in water. Several homes on Golf Drive may catch your eye, especially the multi-gabled Tudor with chimney pots at 6800, built in 1933 for the princely sum of $4,000.

Where Golf runs into Rankin, you'll see a sidewalk curving invitingly past several old cottonwood trees. Follow the sidewalk into Curtis Park. The lake on your right is Curtis Lake. The lake on your left was created by the original owners of the homes here, who dammed the creek so they could have a small lake in their backyards. It was not a city project. This picturesque lake is one of the loveliest in University Park and perhaps has the most wildfowl. Depending on the season you may spot some Canada geese as well as lots of mallards stopping over for a rest from their migrations. This might also be a good place to spot a turtle. You might want to rest here or on a bench beside Curtis Lake and enjoy the tranquility of the scene.

Continue to the right around Curtis Lake toward the stone bridge and the picnic area. When the 1972 bond issue to improve the lakes passed, the walls at Curtis Lake were lowered to permit sloping of the ground surface closer to the water, and the face of the dam was altered to improve its appearance. The old bridge appears to be of WPA vintage. The land where the baseball diamond now stands was once very hilly, but was bulldozed flat in the early fifties.

The area that is now the park was once known as "The Thicket." Two Daniel sisters, granddaughters of pioneer Frances Sims Daniel, lived near here in a semi-log cabin located where the Spanish-style home at 3544 Rankin now stands, south of Curtis Lake. On a Saturday afternoon they would put on their bonnets and walk across the fields all the way to University Grocery located where Culwell and Son is today, at McFarlin and Hillcrest. They would be given a ride back in "The Hack" (a Model-T Ford with a top) unless it was too muddy. Then a football player from SMU would throw the groceries over his shoulder and help them slosh home.

Walk to the right of the picnic area to see the University Park swimming pool. It was built in 1931 using mules and "Fresnos" (large scoops) to dig out the dirt. Later it was enlarged to its Olympic size, and two fill-and-drain pools were added for young children.

Continue past the pool toward the flagpole at the northeast corner of the park. Between the pool and the flagpole you'll pass a giant cottonwood tree and a hackberry tree with labels on their trunks at eye level. In 1938 Curtis Park was named for H. J. Curtis, the third mayor of University Park (1930–1938). A bronze plaque can be found on the base of the flagpole.

Cross to the north side of Lovers Lane and walk west past University Park School, built in 1928 at a cost of $110,000. You can see the date clearly above the main entrance. Its cornerstone provides an interesting mystery. In it were placed some American and foreign coins, copies of Dallas newspapers, and a Bible. But while we know what is supposed to be in the cornerstone, nobody seems to know where the cornerstone is! Can you find it? At any rate, Armstrong School was by then overcrowded and sent pupils and six teachers to the new school. Although an east wing was added in 1933 and a west wing in 1939 to try to keep up with a rapidly developing area, double sessions still had to be held in the forties. Keep in mind that as late as 1940 University Park was north and east of the Dallas city limits. University Park was growing so fast the city was having a hard time providing services to all the new homes. Only the building of a new school in the late forties, Robert S. Hyer, relieved overcrowded classrooms. (See the Hyer-Greenbrier Walk.) University Park School continued to expand in 1950 when the northeast and northwest corners were added. The building was not air-conditioned until 1970. Major landscaping was done in 1981, and the building now boasts a remodeled kindergarten wing.

If you have a sharp eye, you may have noticed on previous walks the markers in the sidewalks. If not, begin to notice at the beginning of a stretch of sidewalk or on a curb that you'll often see "Klein Brothers" and below it the date when that portion of sidewalk was laid, such as 1926. For many years the Klein Brothers were called upon in University Park and Highland Park for their excellent concrete work. Notice how seldom a Klein sidewalk is badly cracked. They also poured the University Park pools.

For an optional extension to your walk, turn right at Thackeray and walk two blocks north to Stanford. (Or simply read the next few paragraphs and continue your walk on the south side of Lovers Lane.) On the southeast corner of the intersection of Thackeray and Stanford was located one of the three artesian wells that were the main water source for the earliest residents of University Park in the early twenties. Later it was abandoned and the pumps were removed. But this area tended to collect water, and in the seventies the city had to haul in several large loads of dirt to fill in the big hole. Just half a block north is Barns Park, landscaped with small, smooth creek stones.

Go back south on Thackeray and turn right on Amherst. On the north side of Amherst midway between Thackeray and Turtle Creek Boulevard is a distinctive home at 3620 Amherst, built over the channelized creek, with statuary in the yard. On the other side of the street, Turtle Creek emerges after its travels underground from Caruth Park. Its flow is slowed after its long trip from its origin, about seven hundred feet north of Walnut Hill Lane near Hillcrest. The creek once meandered through the Hillcrest area and then along what is now Turtle Creek Boulevard, long since paved.

Someone once called this picturesque little lake "Culture Gulch" because Jerry Bywaters, former head of the Dallas Museum of Art, and Lon Tinkle, author and critic, lived in two of the houses here. Both of their homes were designed by architect O'Neil Ford. Some of the homeowners near these lakes used to add fresh water to the creek water to make it cleaner.

Walk back to Thackeray and continue south, then turn right on Lovers Lane to see Culture Gulch from the other

side. Some oldtimers say that Lovers Lane itself used to be a meandering creekbed. Only later did it become a road, lined with bois d'arc trees the Caruth family planted as fence rows. Some of these old trees remain. Billy Daniel of the pioneer Daniel family used to let his cows out in the evening to graze north of Lovers Lane on Caruth land, then bring them back in the morning. On the south side of Lovers Lane, west of the creek, you'll pass under an old leaning bois d'arc tree that has been securely anchored with cables.

If you care to look at a home with a 1988 Park Cities Historical Society marker, continue west on Lovers Lane past Turtle Creek Lane and cross Turtle Creek Boulevard at the light. (Or go ahead and turn south on Turtle Creek Lane.) At 3718 Lovers Lane you'll find another example of David Williams's early style of architecture, Texas Colonial. The two-story brick home built in 1931 was painted white to maintain the colonial tradition as well as to reflect the southern sun. Williams's homes often included some artifact of historical interest, in this case the antique fence and gate salvaged from an old residence in New Orleans.

Retrace your steps on Lovers Lane back to Turtle Creek Boulevard. On the southwest corner of Turtle Creek Boulevard and Lovers Lane, at 7037 Turtle Creek Boulevard, you can see some more interesting ironwork around the home of Mrs. Richard Joseph Potter. Mr. Potter and his father owned Potter Iron Works and added a great deal of beauty in the Park Cities through the iron detailing they created at Highland Park Village, Highland Park Presbyterian Church, Highland Park Methodist Church, and many other Park Cities homes and churches. Their work is also found throughout Dallas and even in such places as Natchez, Mississippi and Williamsburg, Virginia.

Continue across Turtle Creek Boulevard to Turtle Creek Lane and turn south. The peaceful, secluded area you are entering is part of Volk Estates. Most of these stately homes on Turtle Creek Lane were built in the mid-thirties for under $15,000. **As you round the corner to the left onto Turtle Creek Boulevard,** you'll see another historic home at 6930 Turtle Creek that received a Park Cities historical marker in 1988. This informal French Eclectic home has a steeply pitched slate roof with varying roof heights and an off-center doorway. The design has remained unchanged since it was conceived by architect George Dahl. (For more

Albert J. Klein, shown in this 1912 caricature, and his brother J. J. were often hired in University Park and Highland Park to do concrete work. Their markers can still be found in sidewalks throughout the Park Cities. *Courtesy of Lynn Vogt*

on Dahl see the Snider Plaza Walk.) The original driveway was covered with crushed oyster shells brought in from the Gulf Coast. The home, now owned by former University Park mayor Ed Drake (1984–1986), had the distinction when built in 1933 of having one of the first residential swimming pools in the Park Cities.

Continue south on Turtle Creek Boulevard past many impressive homes as you return to Goar Park. If you like to look at homes, this part of the walk is a show stopper, and you'll return to it again in the Volk Estates Walk. On that walk you'll see many examples of informal as well as formal French houses.

Continue south across Goar Park and Williams Park to return to your starting point on McFarlin. The original trickling, wandering Turtle Creek has undergone many changes in the twentieth century, but man has worked with nature to form one of the most beautiful urban creekside areas in the world. Now all that's needed is clean water!

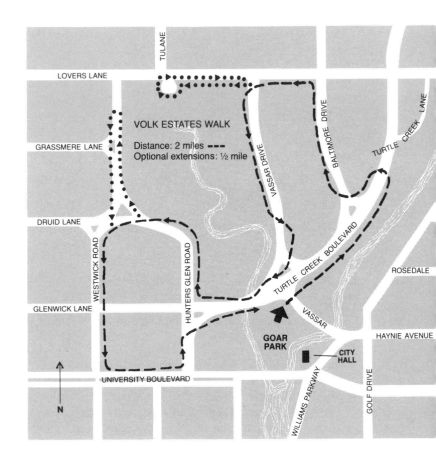

VOLK ESTATES WALK

Distance: 2 miles ---
Optional extensions: ½ mile

LOVERS LANE

TULANE

GRASSMERE LANE

DRUID LANE

GLENWICK LANE

WESTWICK ROAD

HUNTERS GLEN ROAD

VASSAR DRIVE

BALTIMORE DRIVE

TURTLE CREEK LANE

TURTLE CREEK BOULEVARD

ROSEDALE

VASSAR

HAYNIE AVENUE

GOAR PARK

CITY HALL

WILLIAMS PARKWAY

GOLF DRIVE

UNIVERSITY BOULEVARD

N

Volk Estates Walk

*You've waited, NOW BUY. Volk's has split the price on
ladies Oxfords nearly in two—$2.35 for many that sold at
$3.50 and $4.00. A big lot of Oxfords, fine ones, in nearly
complete sizes at $1.95 (these sold at $2.50 to $3.00) and
lots of Strap slippers, in broken, but good sizes, worth
$2.00 to $3.00 at $1.35. Bargains that ARE bargains.*
          —*Beau Monde* magazine, July 1900

VOLK ESTATES was named for Leonard William
Volk, who arrived in Dallas in 1884. Leonard's father
was in the leather business in Baltimore, but there
were too many sons, so Leonard decided to seek his
fortune elsewhere. First he visited Monterrey, Mexico, then Waco, Texas, and finally settled in the
rough-and-ready town of Dallas. There were no paved
streets then, only covered boardwalks in the commercial section. Volk vividly recalled seeing a man thrown
from a second-story window of a saloon shortly after
his arrival in Dallas. Those were not times for the
fainthearted.

With the coming of two railroads that crossed near
Dallas in the 1870s, cotton buyers had flocked to Dallas, which became the main distribution center in
Texas for cotton. Dallas grew so rapidly and lustily
that relentless warfare began between the solid citizens and the gamblers and outlaws. Not until the
turn of the century would the forces of law and order
prevail.

As the decade that came to be known as the Gay
Nineties approached, the chief frontier areas of the
United States had been settled and people were mov-
ing to the cities in record numbers. Electric lights,

football, telephones, phonographs, motion pictures, and even the gasoline automobile all appeared in this rapidly changing society. Fashionable ladies dressed in ankle-length Gibson Girl outfits and furnished their homes in the Victorian style. Actually the Gay Nineties were gay only if you belonged to that one-eighth of the U.S. population that controlled seven-eighths of the U.S. wealth. The rest of the population was struggling to make ends meet and trying to forge a new way of life on the farm or in the city.

Into this setting arrived Leonard Volk, who decided that all these people needed shoes, and who better to provide them than a man skilled in working with leather. After all, the Volk ancestors in Germany had been bootmakers to the King of Bavaria, arriving in the United States around 1837. Leonard persuaded his brother George to join him in Dallas, and together they started Volk Brothers shoe store in 1889. Business prospered and they expanded several times. Their new seven-story downtown store, designed by architect George Dahl, was the first multi-storied building in Dallas to be air-conditioned, with equipment installed by Carrier in 1929. And in 1935 Volk Brothers was the first downtown store to open a suburban outlet, at Highland Park Village.

If Leonard Volk could see the latest developments in the shoe business today, he would be astonished— not just by the prices, but by the huge variety of styles available and by the complicated technology of the industry, especially in the field of athletic shoes. Magazines for runners devote entire issues to reporting the results of elaborate testing procedures on the various shoes. There are special shoes for every sport you can think of, and even dozens of shoes designed specifically for walking. So why don't you pick a comfortable pair of shoes and head for the door?

Volk Estates Walk

A thing of beauty is a joy forever:
Its loveliness increases . . .
  —John Keats, "Endymion"

THERE IS NO question that Volk Estates is one of the most beautiful walks in the Park Cities, with homes that rival those of any other neighborhood. It's a walk you'll want to do again.

If you look on a plat of University Park, you won't find "Volk Estates" listed anywhere but instead will see such names as University Park Estates and Brookside Estates. Yet everyone knows this area as Volk Estates. It's bounded roughly by Lovers Lane, Preston Road, Turtle Creek Boulevard, and University Boulevard.

As you wander among these streets you'll see a variety of architectural styles, secluded tennis courts, picket fences, modern as well as traditional sculpture scattered on manicured lawns, magnificent landscaping, and hidden swimming pools. It's fun to discover some of these sights for yourself. Look for the peacocks strolling on the grounds of one home.

Begin your walk at the intersection of Vassar Drive and Turtle Creek Boulevard, north of Goar Park, and walk northeast on Turtle Creek. Leonard Volk and his brother George opened Volk Brothers shoe store in downtown Dallas in 1889. The business grew and prospered, and by the mid-twenties Leonard decided to invest in a side venture. He bought forty acres of farmland in newly incorporated University Park and with his son Harold, who was born in 1895, began to develop it. Volk's land was bounded by Turtle Creek on the south and east (including Turtle Creek Lane), Lovers Lane on the north, and the creek between Vassar and Hunters Glen on the west. Leonard called his development Brookside Estates. There wasn't a tree in the whole area except for a few by the creek, so he and Harold planted hundreds of trees.

Volk himself lived in the first home in the subdivision, the nicely detailed Tudor home you'll see at 6920 Turtle Creek. It was designed by Hal Thomson and built prior to 1927, and Volk lived here until his death in 1936. His grandson, also called Leonard, remembers coming to visit for Sunday lunch and playing along the creek behind the house, near his grandfather's chipping and putting green. George Charlton, grandson of George Volk, remembers that inside the house at the bottom of the stairs was a suit of armor looking like something out of the movie *Beau Geste*. Notice the enclosed front porch typical of Tudor homes, with a Tudor arch over it. When Tudor homes were first built in England, fireplaces were a new invention. The owners built prominent chimneys to show their neighbors that they could afford the new fireplaces. Even today Tudor homes have massive chimneys, often crowned with decorative chimney pots. Also typically Tudor are steeply pitched cross gables, such as you see here. After Leonard Volk's death, Mr. and Mrs. J. B. O'Hara lived here for a while. It was Mrs. "Pep" O'Hara's father who created the Dr Pepper formula.

Some of the lots in Brookside Estates were vacant for many years, for the Depression hit not long after the project began. Harold F. Volk, Leonard's son, became deeply involved in partitioning the land and putting in streets and utilities, and he had his share of tough times. This was the only development in the Park Cities in which all lots were over an acre. By the early thirties Harold was president of Volk Brothers as well as running the Brookside Development Company. During the Depression he offered double commissions to brokers to sell the lots, but to no avail. So he sold them himself, sometimes getting as little as $3,500 for one of these impressive lots.

Turn back toward the corner of Turtle Creek Boulevard and Baltimore. The home on this corner, one of the original ones in the area, belongs to Lucy Ball Owsley, now in her eighties, who still lives here. Her spectacular French Eclectic house at 6801 Turtle Creek was designed by a man from Cincinnati, John Scudder Adkins, and built of Indiana limestone for Lucy and her husband Alvin in 1929 for $80,000. Notice the high-pitched hipped roof with a slight flare to the eaves and the matching carriage house. Although one might expect such a formal home to have a grand, formal entryway, the front door actually faces the carriage house. Many homes in the Volk Estates have this unusual siting, perhaps done so that visitors could drive right up to the door.

Walk around to the Baltimore side for a better view. For several years before World War II, the Owsleys lived abroad

At the turn of the century *Beau Monde* magazine carried many ads for the popular Volk Brothers shoes. *Courtesy of Dallas Public Library*

6801 Turtle Creek

because Alvin was Envoy Extraordinary and Minister Pleni-
potentiary to Romania, Ireland, and Denmark. When asked
the difference between that and the title of Ambassador, he
replied, "The salary." (A few years later the position he
had held was upgraded to Ambassador.)

Cross the street and begin walking north on Baltimore.
The home at 6801 Baltimore was built by the George T.
Lees in 1929, the same year as the Owsleys' home, for
$30,000. (The prices of homes in this walk are builders' es-
timates found in city records, which, as everyone knows,
are not always the final price.) Lee, whose father had been
Dallas commissioner of streets, was an attorney and a dea-
con of the First Presbyterian Church. Hal Thomson designed the Colonial Revival–style house, originally built
with a flat roof. Mr. Lee himself helped design the incredible Georgian broken pediment and doorway. Notice the
stone used inside the center gable, garlands in the pediment, and keystones over the windows. Center gable sections usually protrude from the house, but this one is
recessed.

Your trip north up Baltimore will bring you to Harold
Volk's first house at 6901, built in 1928, which also has a
semi-side entry. Harold's son, Leonard, remembers a rose
arbor among the tall trees. By 1936 Leonard Sr. had died
and Harold had opened the first suburban branch of a
downtown store in Highland Park Village. People thought

In 1929 the George T. Lees began construction of their new home at 6801 Baltimore. Looking east across Baltimore and Turtle Creek Boulevard, SMU's Dallas Hall is seen in the distance. *Courtesy of Mr. and Mrs. George T. Lee, Jr.*

Northeast across Baltimore from the George T. Lee house under construction is the home being built by Alvin Owsley at 6801 Turtle Creek Boulevard in 1929. *Courtesy of Mr. and Mrs. George T. Lee, Jr.*

he was crazy until his store doubled in size in just a few years, and everyone in the Park Cities was wearing Volk Brothers shoes. His store in the Village had the highest sales volume in the country. The Volks lived in this house on Baltimore until 1936, when they moved into an apartment in the Dallas Country Club for a year or so, then into a duplex until their new home was finished on Vassar in 1940.

Continue north on Baltimore past the home at 6916 Baltimore with Neoclassical columns and Georgian detailing built in 1950. The house at 7000 Baltimore was also built in the early fifties in a very different style, Creole Revival. At 7001 you'll find a "modern" house with strong Frank Lloyd Wright influence.

Turn left at Lovers Lane and walk west to Vassar Drive. The naming of streets in Volk Estates followed the University Park tradition of using names of colleges and universities. **For an optional side trip, continue past Vassar on Lovers Lane until you come to a cul-de-sac with several homes on the south side of Lovers Lane, across from Tulane Boulevard. (Or you can go ahead and turn south on Vassar.)** On your way to the cul-de-sac on Lovers Lane you'll pass a giant old hackberry tree, perhaps the biggest one you've ever seen. At the south end of the cul-de-sac the creek emerges after its long captivity underground (north of Lovers Lane the creek is paved over as Tulane Boulevard). The creek then meanders behind the homes between Vassar and Hunters Glen on its way to the lake at Williams Park and beyond. **As you return to Vassar,** notice the Tudor detailing and stained glass windows on the home designed by Anton Korn at 3900 Lovers Lane.

Turn on Vassar and walk south toward Turtle Creek Boulevard. Don't miss another Tudor home on Vassar Drive at 7037 with patterned brickwork on the front-facing gable. It was built by Mr. and Mrs. Cecil Higginbotham of Higginbotham & Bailey Dry Goods Company in 1934 for $15,000. Tudor houses originally used windows with small panes because big panes of glass weren't being made. Even though this had changed by the 1920s, people still used tiny leaded glass panes to look like the old Tudor homes. Take note of the slightly colored panes of the window on the left (pale pink, turquoise) mixed with white panes in a random pattern. Also notice that this is a stone house with brickwork around the windows. This is unusual, as most

Tudor houses are made of brick with stonework around the windows.

Directly across the street at 7000 Vassar is the home completed by Harold Volk in 1940, the first contemporary house that I. Gayden Thompson designed. There are Chinese references in the geometrical detailing. The two huge red oak trees on either side of the lot, and many of the other trees, were planted by Mrs. Dorothy Volk. Including the Volk family, there were forty-eight children in the neighborhood during the forties. One large tree on the back of the lot was a popular hangout for the neighborhood children because of the treehouse in its branches. Sharing joys, surviving traumas, the neighbors of Volk Estates became a close-knit group of friends raising families, gathering on Christmas Day at one home or another to celebrate the holiday season.

During 1949 Volk Brothers built a second suburban store at Live Oak and Skillman. By then Volk Brothers had become more than a shoe store, selling clothes and gifts as well. In 1969 Harold sold his business to his vice president who then sold it a year later to Colbert's with the agreement that Colbert's could use Volk's name for a certain period of time. Harold died in 1979.

Dr. and Mrs. George Aldredge live in the house at 6928 Vassar, where they raised nine children. A former owner of the home, Jack Munger, was the grandson of one of the developers of Munger Place (a housing development in East Dallas that opened in 1905 and was instantly successful). After Jack Munger, the home was owned by Fenton Baker, who managed the Baker Hotel (built in 1924 and, along with the Adolphus, one of the two premier hotels in Dallas).

Harold and Dorothy Volk's neighbor for many years at 6909 Vassar (designed by Fooshee and Cheek and built in 1933) was the colorful David Harold ("Dry Hole") Byrd, who drilled fifty-six dry holes before becoming a successful oilman. One of the first men to buy leases in the East Texas oil field, Byrd was the cousin of Admiral Byrd, famous for his Antarctic explorations. In 1935 he married into a prominent family when he married Mattie Caruth, granddaughter of William Caruth who had arrived in Dallas in 1848. (See the Caruth Walk.) The Byrd home was the site of many fabulous parties, including the famous annual party on the night of the Texas-Oklahoma football game.

Among hundreds of other guests, the entire Texas band was invited. Barrels of oysters were served, as well as buffalo, antelope, and bear, for Byrd was an avid hunter. He had a gigantic white polar bear standing in the corner to prove it! His next-door neighbor at 6905 Vassar, Dick Bass, is an avid mountaineer who has climbed Mount Everest and the highest peak on each continent.

Mattie Byrd was well-known for her generosity in providing funds for University Park publications, and upon her death she willed her half of the Byrd Estate to the city. Anyone who knows the value of these properties today realizes what a benevolent gift she bequeathed. Speaking of gifts to University Park, the triangles of land you see along Turtle Creek Boulevard were deeded to the city by Leonard Volk, Sr., and yet it is interesting that none bears his name.

Be sure to see the tower on the garage of the home at 6701 Turtle Creek, east of Vassar just across from the triangle where Vassar splits in two. This superb Norman French house was built in 1928. One of the first owners was E. L. DeGolyer, wealthy oilman and philanthropist, who later built an estate on forty-three acres at White Rock Lake which has become the Dallas Arboretum, and for whom the DeGolyer Library at Southern Methodist University is named. A subsequent owner was J. A. R. Moseley, whose wife was a Wadley. When their seven-year-old son died of leukemia, she started the Wadley Blood Bank. The house is currently owned by the Henry Billingsleys. Lucy Billingsley is the daughter of Trammell Crow, famed real estate developer. Although less formal than the Owsley house, the Billingsley house has the same high-pitched roof and slight flare to the eaves. It is modeled after a French country house. The recent brickwork around the lot ties it in with the triangle.

Walk over to the triangle at Vassar and Turtle Creek to see the two bronze markers, one at the southwest corner and one below the statue. The triangle was named Byrd Parkway in 1983 when the Byrd Foundation funded its beautification. But the money for the statue was given by Trammell and Margaret Crow in honor of their grandchildren. The horse is named Huipago.

Walk west on Turtle Creek Boulevard toward Hunters Glen. At 6600 Turtle Creek, note the original front door and the stonework on the house, which has not been painted over, so the Tudor detailing is still visible.

An aerial photograph of the George T. Lee home at 6801 Baltimore shows the original flat roof. In the upper left corner is the Norman French–style home at 6701 Turtle Creek. *Courtesy of Mr. and Mrs. George T. Lee, Jr.*

Perhaps the heart of the Volk Estates today is the land between Vassar and Hunters Glen where a branch of Turtle Creek flows on its way to the Trinity River through University Park and Highland Park. Because the lots around the creek are much larger and even more wooded than the other lots in the area, these homes can aptly be called estates.

The estate at 6601 Turtle Creek, encircled by hedges and red oak trees, is the largest piece of residential property in University Park. The home, designed by Anton Korn and built in 1931, was for many years the residence of multimillionaire oilman, philanthropist, and SMU benefactor Algur H. Meadows. Nearby at 6525 Turtle Creek lived Fred Florence, "Mr. Republic Bank," who became Meadows's close friend as well as business associate. (The Florence house has been torn down and the land replatted; there is no 6525 now.) Annual neighborhood Christmas parties were held in Meadows's red brick Tudor home, which has since been extensively remodeled by architect Wilson McClure. Meadows died in a tragic traffic accident. In 1981 the property was bought by a California developer who wanted to divide the land into three lots. Because neighbors objected, the city council, acting upon the advice of the planning and zoning commission, regretfully rejected the proposal, realizing it meant a loss of tax revenues. But in doing so they preserved something special about University Park.

When Volk and other developers bought this farmland in the twenties, University Park was simply a small university town. Most of the residents were young SMU professors with lots of children, certainly not an affluent crowd. The wealthy families moving into this development around Turtle Creek gave the city distinction, and so it remains today.

Funds for the landscaping of the small triangle at Hunters Glen were given in 1983 by the Meadows Foundation, the largest private foundation in Texas, requesting that the triangle be named the Meadows-Florence Park in memory of the two University Park friends and neighbors. The Meadows School of the Arts and Florence Hall at SMU are named for them also. Before turning on Hunters Glen, glance south to see the Gothic spire, gables, and stained glass windows of the Highland Park Presbyterian Church at the end of Turtle Creek Boulevard.

Walk north on Hunters Glen, which leads you into the development originally called University Park Estates. The Colonial Revival mansion ahead at 6601 Hunters Glen was built in 1931 by Cullen F. Thomas, lawyer and Baylor benefactor. The north wing added later was matched extremely well. Take note of the Adam style fanlight over the door, the window surrounds, and quoins. The home may look familiar to fans of the TV show "Dallas." Its former owners allowed the home to be filmed in early episodes.

The house at 6700 Hunters Glen, built in 1936, is an example of a style that was constructed for a brief period during the thirties and forties. It's a variation of the Monterey Revival style called Creole Revival because the balcony columns and balustrades are of wrought iron instead of wood, giving it a New Orleans touch. Very few homes like this one were built, since few people could afford them during the Depression. Their popularity waned in the next decade.

In fact, all of the houses erected in Volk Estates as well as in Highland Park West and Loma Linda during the thirties are really unique on a national scale. Dallas was a wealthy city because the discovery of the East Texas oil field brought big influxes of cash into town via the banking system. Many home styles found in the pattern books of the thirties which you see in the Park Cities will not be found in other areas of the country.

For an optional side trip, pass Druid Lane and continue north on Hunters Glen a block and a half. (Or you can

simply read this paragraph and continue.) At 6915 Hunters Glen you'll find a unique eclectic Spanish Colonial home set back on the lot. The stone house, designed by architects Flint and Broad, was built in 1936 and was given a Park Cities Historical Society marker in 1988. Notice the brickwork around the windows and the typical low-pitched red tile roof. The south wing was added in 1972.

Retrace your steps to Druid Lane. At 3925 Druid Lane is a French Eclectic mansion with a high pitched roof, very elaborate door surround, and tiny dormers with curved tops. Volk Estates has more French Eclectic homes, both formal ones like the Owsleys' and informal ones like the Billingsleys', than any other part of the Park Cities.

Where Hunters Glen, Druid Lane, and Westwick merge, head south on Westwick toward University Boulevard. You'll pass another outstanding French Eclectic house at 3941 Glenwick, on the southeast corner of the intersection of Westwick and Glenwick. Recently built, it is indicative of a trend in the last ten years toward building period homes. Its original owners studied French architecture and design in Paris before building it.

Turn left at University and walk east. On the northeast corner of the intersection at 3928 University is a well-preserved home built in 1925. The front door appears to be original, and the pecan trees in front are probably as old as the house. Note the mix of house styles as you continue east on University to Turtle Creek.

Turn left on Turtle Creek to return to your starting point. Leonard Volk, standing on the boardwalk in Dallas in 1884, probably never dreamed how much pleasure and prestige his side venture of a housing development would someday bring to University Park. Having walked Volk Estates, you'll probably agree it's a "thing of beauty" that seems to be growing increasingly lovely with age as the sapling trees have matured and spread their shade over the picturesque mansions nestled on green lawns amidst curving streets. Did you find the peacocks?

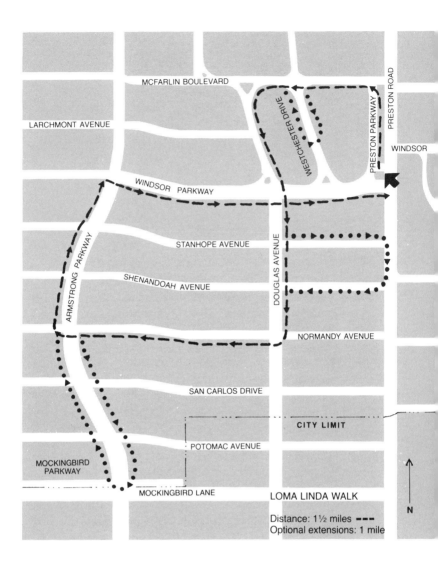

MCFARLIN BOULEVARD

LARCHMONT AVENUE

PRESTON ROAD

PRESTON PARKWAY

WESTCHESTER DRIVE

WINDSOR

WINDSOR PARKWAY

ARMSTRONG PARKWAY

STANHOPE AVENUE

DOUGLAS AVENUE

SHENANDOAH AVENUE

NORMANDY AVENUE

SAN CARLOS DRIVE

CITY LIMIT

POTOMAC AVENUE

MOCKINGBIRD
PARKWAY

MOCKINGBIRD LANE

LOMA LINDA WALK

Distance: 1½ miles ---
Optional extensions: 1 mile

N

Loma Linda Walk

LOMA LINDA's development began during that colorful decade of shocking morals and soaring stock profits, the Roaring Twenties. In many ways the 1920s were a turning point in the United States. For the first time in our history, more people lived in cities than in the country, and one housing development after another was created to house them. Spectacular economic growth encouraged many new investors in the stock market and widespread speculation in business. The Nineteenth Amendment and its right to vote seemed to give women a new zest for life, which expressed itself in radical new clothing fashions and "bobbed" hairstyles.

The number of cars in the U.S. tripled, and "flappers" and "beaus" sped past these Loma Linda walls in their new automobiles wearing raccoon coats, on their way to visit speakeasies where they drank bootleg liquor, danced the Charleston, and listened to jazz, the latest craze in music. The prohibition amendment made breaking the law fashionable. Never mind that in a few years this euphoria would all come crashing down, for Americans didn't want to listen, so immersed were they in forgetting their European troubles. Hadn't World War I been, as Woodrow Wilson claimed, the "war to end all wars"? What better cause for a nationwide celebration?

This was a time of heroes as Jack Dempsey boxed his way to fame, Babe Ruth slugged a record number of baseballs out of the ballpark, and Charles Lindbergh captured the imagination of the world with his first solo flight across the Atlantic. Anything was possible.

These liberated ladies of the Roaring Twenties riding in a Packard are celebrating July Fourth and possibly their right to vote as well.

This was also a time of characters. Charlie Chaplin delighted his audiences by portraying a little tramp shuffling across the silent screen in baggy britches, diminutive coat, and battered derby hat. Families would gather around the radio in the evenings to chuckle over the latest antics of "Amos 'n Andy."

And the Loma Linda development had its own set of characters, even mavericks, responsible for its birth during this fast-paced era, men as colorful as the development they helped to create.

Loma Linda Walk

TO SAMPLE a portion of the Loma Linda area, begin your walk on Preston Parkway just off Preston Road, at the intersection of Windsor Parkway. You'll find a cool, covered bench, decorated with Spanish tiles, on which

to sit and read a little of its history before embarking on your walk.

Architect David Williams designed the Loma Linda walls and gateways. He and his twin brother were born on the Texas frontier in the late nineteenth century in a settlement of dugouts that would become Childress. An outgoing, adventurous man, Williams had worked in Mexico and had several narrow escapes during the Mexican Revolution. After a brief tour of Europe during which he collected rare books, prints, and even unusual hats (which he insisted everyone wear when he had a party), he settled in Dallas. Soon Williams was asked to design an area called Greenway Parks where he created a park-living design, with homes built around a common green, that was as innovative as it was beautiful. This was the first time a pedestrian-oriented neighborhood had been tried in Dallas, and it remains relatively unchanged today. (Greenway Parks is located between Mockingbird and University just west of the Tollway.)

But while Greenway Parks was developed from land that had been a large farm, Loma Linda would be developed on a parcel of land that had been deeded to the Catholic church for one dollar. Finances were a continuing concern for the Vincentian order of the Catholic church, which provides for their fathers who take a vow of poverty as well as for their schools and churches. In 1905 the Vincentians had founded Holy Trinity University, with a building designed by H. A. Overbeck, located at Oak Lawn and Blackburn (where Jesuit High School was later located and where Turtle Creek Village now stands). In 1910 they changed the name to Dallas University, stealing the idea from Dr. Robert S. Hyer, who had publicly stated just the week before that the new Methodist university on Hillcrest (now Southern Methodist University) should have that name. To help with the financing of the Catholics' new university, a benefactor named John J. LeSage, who was also a Vincentian father, deeded a fifty-six-acre parcel of land for one dollar to Dallas University. (In the 1940s the university would become bankrupt and be revived under a different Catholic order in Irving in the 1950s as the University of Dallas.)

Father Finney was the president of Dallas University as well as the first pastor of the Holy Trinity Church across the street. The gift of land the church received from LeSage was bounded by Preston Road on the east, the Cotton Belt Railroad (now the Dallas North Tollway) on the west, University Boulevard on the north, and Mockingbird Lane and the border of Highland Park on the south. During the postwar surge of growth, Father Finney concluded that this land could be subdivided and sold, providing needed church finances, especially if the development rode on the coattails of Highland Park West's success. Edgar Flippen of Flippen-Prather Realty Company had recently announced to the press that Highland Park West would open soon and, in his words, "the plans for its improvement, development and maintenance will be more elaborate and on a higher plane than anything ever attempted in Texas."

In a letter, Father Finney persuaded Bishop Lynch that a development next to "the highest class residential district in the state" was bound to succeed. The church gave Finney permission to proceed. Having seen Greenway Parks, Father Finney came to David Williams to ask if he could design the layout for another development that would be called Loma Linda, a Spanish name meaning "pretty hill." Since the Greenway Parks lots weren't selling as quickly as

This 1905 photo shows Holy Trinity University just after construction. It was renamed Dallas University in 1910, later became Jesuit High School, and was torn down in 1963. The Loma Linda area of University Park was developed to earn money to help support Dallas University as well as other Catholic church projects. *Courtesy of the Dallas Public Library*

its investors had hoped, Williams laid out the church's development in a more conservative modified-grid pattern.

The developers of Loma Linda wanted something to attract the attention of the many passing motorists on Preston and Mockingbird and to draw them to this community. The solution, built in 1924, was a set of low brick walls of Spanish design, with elaborate gateways covered with brightly colored decorative tile, which can be seen now on Preston as well as on Mockingbird. In later years when Williams became known for his indigenous Texas style of architecture, he was actually embarrassed that he had designed them. Yet these colorful walls were a perfect expression of the time in which they were conceived, the fast-paced Roaring Twenties. In the early thirties, Highland Park would pick up this Spanish theme again in its shopping development a few blocks away, the Highland Park Village.

Take time to look closely at the walls and gateways, with twisted columns indicating Moorish influence, red tile roofing, and even a ceramic vase or two. Not only do they provide a visual entryway into an elegant neighborhood, but they also help to buffer the noise of the traffic. At one time the City of University Park considered removing the words "Loma Linda" on the Mockingbird walls and inserting "University Park," though fortunately the historic name of the walls was preserved. The walls have been a source of pride to University Park, which was incorporated in the same year they were built and later annexed the development. Loma Linda is a unique neighborhood with a Spanish name, bounded by Spanish Colonial Revival walls, in

which all the streets were said originally to have had Spanish names. Only two of those names remain, San Carlos ("St. Charles") and Lomo Alto ("high hill"), which in more correct Spanish should read "Loma Alta."

Walk north along Preston Parkway to McFarlin. The first house on Preston Parkway was built before 1928 at 6315 in Spanish Eclectic style with a red tile roof to blend with the character of the walls behind which it was built. The roof has been changed, but the Spanish doorway and rounded arches betray its original style.

Houses began to spring up almost immediately in the Loma Linda area, and people of distinction began to move into the neighborhood. In 1936 Roy Coffee, Sr., built his dream home at 6325 Preston Parkway, where he would live for many years. Solidly built of steel and concrete, his Tudor-style mansion should stand for generations to come. Typical of Tudor design is the brickwork with stone around the windows; the home's symmetrical design, however, is unusual. Coffee became mayor of University Park (1950–1970), as did his son after him (1976–1982). When the house changed owners in 1980, it was chosen as a Dallas Symphony Showcase home.

Turn left at McFarlin and walk west, as you cast a last glance at the Loma Linda walls. The Church of Christ on the corner was built in 1950 on Loma Linda land where an old home had been. The church had to get a variance from the City of University Park because their building is not set back as far from Preston as those on Preston Parkway.

For an optional side trip, turn left on Westchester and walk half a block south to see several noteworthy homes. Among these is another Tudor home with patterned windows at 6325 Westchester, a Spanish Eclectic house with textured stucco and an unusual doorway at 6315, and a Colonial Revival with an Adam fanlight at 6314.

Return to McFarlin and continue west to see a cluster of Tudor houses. After World War I, Prairie-style and Craftsman-style homes such as found in the first Highland Park neighborhoods were out of vogue. Period dwellings became popular choices in the Loma Linda area as well as in Highland Park West, which opened in the same year, 1924. Combinations of styles were rare. Only later would architects and builders begin to experiment with mixtures of Tudor, Spanish, and Colonial Revival influences.

At 4200 McFarlin you'll find a late Tudor home, built in 1931, with tabs emerging around the windows. The house at 4205 McFarlin, built in 1928, later became the home of oilman and philanthropist Herbert Hunt. Before turning left on Douglas, continue past the Tudor home at 4214 McFarlin as far as the driveway to view this bricklayer's delight (or nightmare), an ornate Tudor house with several chimneys, including a decorative double chimney with chimney pots on the west side. In just a few blocks you'll see several more bricklayer's delights when you arrive at a series of homes of an entirely different style, all designed by another character involved with the development of Loma Linda, Charles Dilbeck.

Turn left and walk south on Douglas. Take note of a very unusual home at 6308 Douglas, which pattern books of the day called an English Regency design with its low roof and octagonal windows. Look for the Greek key motif around the roof.

Winding streets and varied landscaping offer continually changing views. At the intersection of Windsor Parkway and Douglas two Spanish Eclectic houses catch your eye, especially one in a bright pink color. They blend well with the picturesque character of the neighborhood created by David Williams.

Williams and his partner, O'Neil Ford, were considered mavericks and even eccentrics in the late twenties. For several years Williams had designed period houses, especially those of Spanish influence. Then, instead of building the popular English, French, Spanish, or Italian mansions you see here and in Highland Park West, they began creating unique regionally oriented Texas homes. (See the Turtle Creek Walk and the Preston Road Walk.)

Continue south across Windsor Parkway to Stanhope. A few years later another maverick, Charles Dilbeck, arrived on the scene to create another kind of regional home in an inimitable style, more sprawling and informal than that of Williams. No pattern books contain these designs, for there are no two exactly alike. A perfect example of that is found east of Douglas on Stanhope, where two very different houses standing side by side, 4140 and 4144 Stanhope, were both designed by Dilbeck. **An optional extension to your walk will take you east on Stanhope past two more Dilbecks at 4105 and 4101 Stanhope, then south on**

Preston under the spreading arms of a sycamore tree to Shenandoah, and west on Shenandoah back to Douglas. (Or you can simply continue south on Douglas.)

At the intersection of Shenandoah and Douglas, you'll find examples of Dilbeck's work on all four corners. Like all his hybrid creations, these homes contain a mixture of natural materials including brick, stone, stucco, and wood combined in whimsical ways. The results are warm, almost rustic cottages with elaborate chimneys, towers or cupolas protruding in odd places, waving designs in brickwork or shingles, surprises wherever you look.

Charles S. Dilbeck was born in Arkansas in 1907 and by the time he was a teenager had already designed and built at least one building. After studying architecture in college for two years, he began designing period homes for Tulsa oil barons. The Depression brought Dilbeck to Dallas, where he located his office in the recently opened Highland Park Village in 1932.

By 1934 he had built the home at 4144 Shenandoah, which the neighbors call "the house with the crooked shutter" because of the intentionally crookedly-hung shutter on the guest suite next to the garage. The restored roof is heavy, hand-split cedar shakes put on in a carefully irregular pattern to resemble the first roof. The paint on the stone and brick has been sandblasted to reveal the original character. Some have called this a Norman French design. The patios and walkways that have been added enhance the house, which was awarded a Park Cities historical marker in 1987.

As you look at the Spanish-flavor Dilbeck home at 4200 Shenandoah, note the brickwork cantilevered out from a window and then carried out in the brick pattern around the porch. Each of his homes has a few unique features, as well as certain similarities. See if you can discover them. Dilbeck is now retired and lives in a home he designed in the late sixties at 3501 Cornell, which on the outside hardly resembles his earlier work. If you'd like to see more Dilbeck homes, the 4000 block of Bryn Mawr is filled with his work, from the waving roof at 4001 to the house at 4085 that he built as his first home and used for a time as his office as well.

Continue south on Douglas to Normandy, then turn right on Normandy and walk west to Armstrong Parkway.

In the 4200 and 4300 block of Normandy you'll see a series of duplexes, smaller in scale than the homes on Preston Parkway and Windsor. While this neighborhood is by no means poor, it doesn't reflect the wealth of other parts of Loma Linda. If "poverty is preservation's friend," as a historical society leader once said, then perhaps it is fortunate that the owners of these duplexes haven't had the means, or the desire, to alter them from their original form. Thus a slice of time has remained for us to view, for nearly all these structures were built in 1929, 1930, and 1931, using the yellow brick common at the beginning of the Depression.

If you choose to extend your walk to Mockingbird to see the other half of the Loma Linda walls, swing left on Armstrong Parkway and walk south across San Carlos and Potomac to Mockingbird. (Or you can go ahead and turn north on Armstrong.) The first homes in the church's development were actually built on San Carlos, Potomac, and Mockingbird, at least a dozen by 1926. Because of the Depression and later World War II, Loma Linda was not completely developed for many years.

As you return north on Armstrong and east on Windsor Parkway to where your walk began, imagine these streets as they were after World War I. No longer do we see Stutz

Bearcats speeding past or hear the music of composer George Gershwin wafting by in the breeze on warm evenings. That small airplane buzzing overhead has become a jet taking off from Love Field with a deafening roar at the expense of our ears. The small saplings planted on the former cotton fields have grown into mature trees, just as skyscrapers have sprouted on Dallas's skyline.

The Catholic church, along with several maverick designers, has left its mark on University Park with a refreshing development as colorful as it is varied, an eloquent reminder of a bygone era, the Roaring Twenties.

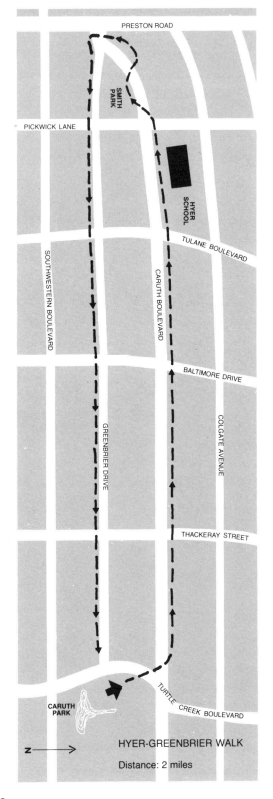

PRESTON ROAD

SMITH PARK

PICKWICK LANE

HYER SCHOOL

TULANE BOULEVARD

SOUTHWESTERN BOULEVARD

CARUTH BOULEVARD

BALTIMORE DRIVE

COLGATE AVENUE

GREENBRIER DRIVE

THACKERAY STREET

CARUTH PARK

TURTLE CREEK BOULEVARD

N →

HYER-GREENBRIER WALK

Distance: 2 miles

Hyer-Greenbrier Walk

UNTIL the twentieth century, most Americans lived on farms or on the frontier, toiling from dawn to dusk to obtain the basic necessities of life, food and shelter. Several pioneers in the history of the Park Cities had large farms—among these the Caruths, the Coles, and the Daniels. As we have seen in the Daniel Cemetery Walk, nature took its toll on these hardworking pioneers. But by 1920 people had begun flocking to the cities, and for the first time in our history more than 50 percent of Americans lived in an urban environment. After World War II the growth of cities was nothing short of phenomenal. Neighborhoods such as the ones you are about to walk sprang up almost overnight.

The growing middle class who lived here began to work shorter hours yet at the same time to receive enough pay so that at least a small portion was left over after the basic necessities were provided. The resulting leisure time—and the issue of what to do with it—is a relatively modern phenomenon that affects us all to some extent. The question many people are beginning to ask is not "How are we going to make a living?" but "How are we going to live?"

This new freedom is a double-edged sword that offers rich possibilities but brings with it a measure of insecurity. For some people, it becomes a major task to determine their goals in life and exactly how they want to spend the time and money so assiduously accumulated. These are no small decisions. Days can loom ahead in dreary emptiness, or they can be filled with new interests and challenges.

There's a Russian poem by Rasul Rza that says it well:

> *The hours slip past;*
> *our moments melt*
> *into the eternity behind us;*
> *Time sweeps us on*
> *to a destination*
> *from which there is no return. . . .*
> *While yet there is time*
> *look out upon the world*
> *devour it with your eyes,*
> *and, if your spirit demands more,*
> *add at least one stone*
> *to the edifice being built.*
> *Fill your lungs with the smell of flowers;*
> *let the first cool breath of dawn*
> *blow through your hair . . .*
> *While yet there is time*
> *live,*
> *labor,*
> *but live and labor*
>   *so that when you are gone*
> *everyone will see*
> *that where once you were*
> *an emptiness yawns.*

While you walk through the Hyer-Greenbrier area and other unique neighborhoods in the Park Cities, you may want to ponder your own heritage and take stock of your own goals in life. As Thoreau said, it is not enough to be busy. The question is, what are we busy about?

Hyer-Greenbrier Walk

THE BEST place to begin your walk is on Turtle Creek Boulevard on the west side of Caruth Park. The land for the park was given by the Caruths in 1929, but in part due to the Depression years, little was here until the late thirties except the creek, very few trees, and some open space. Then WPA labor built the sandstone structures, a tennis court and sidewalks were added, and Caruth Park began to take the shape you see today. (See also the Caruth Walk.)

Walk up to the corner of Caruth Boulevard and turn left to walk west on Caruth. By the late thirties University Park development had reached north to Southwestern, and there were several blocks of houses on Greenbrier. But there were no homes as far north as Caruth. It is important to realize that these homes on Caruth were built for the most part after World War II. What steel and other materials were available during the war were used for the war effort. Not until 1947–48 did building begin again in earnest, and the extraordinary results are here for you to see. By this time University Park had strict zoning ordinances, evidenced by the uniformity of lot sizes and the relative consistency in size and appearance of the houses.

Caruth Boulevard is an extra-wide street because it was planned as the main east/west artery. But Southwestern became the main artery instead, and a boulevard was never built on Caruth, leaving its lot sizes and parkways larger than those on neighboring streets.

By the 1940s University Park School was already bursting at the seams and was having double sessions to try to educate all the children. The war effort had also slowed plans for Robert S. Hyer School, which was to have been built in 1941. By the time it actually was built and opened in 1949, there were already 270 children in the neighborhood.

Seven and one-half acres of land had been purchased in the early thirties for the purpose of building Hyer School. The land was bounded by Caruth, Colgate, Pickwick, and a creek on the east where Tulane is today. Homeowners near Tulane will tell you that raccoons and other creatures still make regular appearances out of the storm sewers beneath Tulane, probably wondering what happened to their beautiful creek. As anyone who has built a home here recently can attest, it is only a few feet down until one strikes the water table. It can be as deep as twenty feet before hitting bedrock, limestone, or Austin chalk, deposited millions of years ago when this area was part of the ocean.

Continue west on Caruth until you come to Hyer School, between Tulane and Pickwick. Even if you didn't know a creek had been there, the giant cottonwood tree that the sidewalk curves around on the southeast corner of Hyer School grounds tells you that water is nearby. Although not as old as the famed pecan tree in Highland Park— cottonwood trees don't get that old—its size indicates that it's one of the oldest cottonwoods in the Park Cities. A number of live oak trees have been planted all the way around Hyer School, each one donated by a graduating class. As you walk past the school, look for the bronze markers set in the ground a short distance from each tree indicating which class donated it. The rose bushes on the wire fence were donated by the Girl Scouts.

Construction actually began in 1947 on the building, but the first classes were not held until January of 1949. The bronze plaque just inside the front entrance shows the date 1947–49. The building, designed by architect Mark Lemmon, cost $408,000. It became the sixth and last school to be built by the Highland Park Independent School District. Now that Dallas has surrounded the Park Cities and the boundaries of the cities are fixed, the population is not likely to fluctuate widely. In 1950 the census showed that the population of University Park had peaked at 23,823. By 1980 the count was 22,254. Though the population is lower now, there are more houses than ever before, which must mean that families are getting smaller.

The first principal of Hyer School was Newton L. Manning, a "native son" who had been a grocery clerk at University Grocery on Hillcrest when he was a boy. As principal he stole the hearts of all the Hyer children by bringing chickens, goats, and other animals to school for them to see. The farmlands and fields that had once dotted the area were fast disappearing, and children had fewer opportunities to see these animals. In 1939 University Park had banned the keeping of cows, goats, hogs, and horses.

The school was named to honor Dr. Robert Stewart Hyer, a pioneer in education in Texas. He was president of Southwestern University in Georgetown, Texas, from 1898 to 1911. But he is best remembered as the man who made

When Hyer School opened at 3920 Caruth Boulevard in January 1949, students and teachers walked from University Park School carrying their books and equipment. *Courtesy of Arles Bynum*

Newton L. Manning, beloved first principal of Hyer School, is shown here holding a black baby goat named Sunshine, with students Gary Marlow and Lisa Crook. *Courtesy of Hyer Elementary School*

227

the dream of Southern Methodist University a reality. He spearheaded its founding and became its first president from 1911 to 1920. Hyer supervised the raising of funds for SMU, meanwhile approving architectural plans for the new buildings, recruiting a faculty, developing a curriculum, acquiring laboratory equipment, and starting a library. After 1920 Hyer became president emeritus and a professor of physics. He died in 1929, never knowing that a school would be named for him.

Beyond Hyer School on the south side of Caruth is another of the city's parks, Smith Park, begun in 1942 and named for J. Fred Smith, first mayor of University Park (1924–1928). Notice the bronze plaque on the WPA-built flagpole. Until the seventies this was simply a landscaped area with a few trees and some bushes. The tennis courts and play equipment were added later.

Across the street from the park is University Park United Methodist Church, whose first building formally opened in 1942 with not much around it but plowed fields. The nearest homes were on the other side of Preston Road. And across from the church was the newly dedicated, freshly landscaped Smith Park.

In 1939 SMU and W. W. Caruth, Sr., gave four lots at Preston Road and Caruth for this new church building, and later deeded a fifth lot. Highland Park Methodist Church and others contributed money toward the founding of the new church. The new members rented Highland Park High School on Sunday mornings for thirty dollars per month. Plans for building the new church were underway when the Japanese attack on Pearl Harbor, December 7, 1941, brought drastic changes. Because of the shortage of steel and other materials, plans for a two-story, fireproof building were replaced by a one-story structure. The first sanctuary opened in 1942.

After the war, the congregation went to work on building a new sanctuary, which officially opened in 1950. Notice the cornerstone dated 1949 near Preston Road. Then in 1955 the new $675,000 education wing was built at the corner of Caruth and Pickwick. The wartime sanctuary building, located in the middle of the complex, had become the fellowship hall, but the termites were waging their own war on it. In 1975 the church completed the work the termites had begun and tore down the old sanctuary, replacing it with the new fellowship center. All the build-

This photograph of Preston Road several blocks south of the church was taken in January 1941. The photographer must have been perched on a ladder between Stanford and Purdue, facing south. *Courtesy of First RepublicBank Park Cities*

ings were then artfully tied together with brickwork and landscaping.

Cross over to the landscaped area on the southeast corner of Greenbrier on Preston Road. This little park was a present to Mrs. E. Wilson Germany from her husband, who was mayor of University Park at the time. He had the area completely landscaped, but the bronze marker was not installed until the day of her birthday, when he brought her to see it. Her present, Greenbrier Park, has been here for all to enjoy ever since that day in 1972.

Walk east on Greenbrier back to Turtle Creek Boulevard to return to Caruth Park. In the late thirties the only blocks on Greenbrier that had houses were the 3500 block and the 3600 block. University Park had not issued a strict zoning ordinance yet, so as you walk along you'll notice a mixture of homes—not just the mix of old and new, but also that of smaller homes built in the late thirties with a few magnificent larger homes that are also fifty years old and still beautiful today. The character of this street is quite different from what you saw at the beginning of your walk on Caruth, just one block north, built in the late forties. Yet each street has its own charm.

This aerial photo of University Park in 1930 shows that only about three or four streets have developed north of Lovers Lane, the street crossing left to right across the middle of the photo. Turtle Creek Boulevard winds through Volk Estates and crosses Lovers Lane. *Courtesy of the City of University Park*

By 1939 this aerial photo shows that development has spread north to Southwestern and to a few blocks on Greenbrier, but no houses have been built as far north as Caruth. *Courtesy of the City of University Park*

In the year 1937 the very first houses to be built on Greenbrier sprang up almost simultaneously. There were still no houses as far north as Caruth. The oldest house is probably the one at 3600, just three months older than the one built by SMU professor Dr. Frank Rader at 3500, across from Caruth Park. At that time the street's name was Quentin Street. Rader went to the city council and told them that he didn't like the name because it sounded too much like a prison, San Quentin. The city council suggested that he get a petition signed by all his neighbors on Quentin Street agreeing to a name change, and then they would act on it. Since there were only a few neighbors, Rader's job was easy. He chose the name Greenbrier because it was the name of his home town in Virginia. The original records at the University Park City Hall show the name Quentin Street marked out by hand and Greenbrier written over it.

Coincidentally, those who live on Greenbrier are all too familiar with a thorny vine that can stick your fingers even through gloves when you try to pull it up by hand. You may even see it growing unwanted out of the landscaping as you walk along. This extremely tenacious, thorny vine is also called "greenbrier."

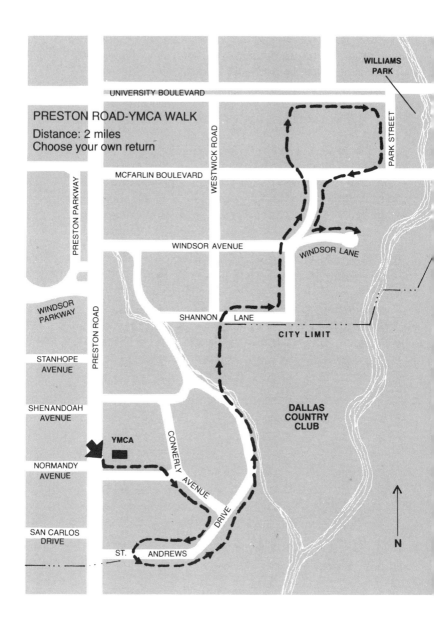

PRESTON ROAD-YMCA WALK

Distance: 2 miles
Choose your own return

WILLIAMS PARK

UNIVERSITY BOULEVARD

WESTWICK ROAD

PARK STREET

MCFARLIN BOULEVARD

PRESTON PARKWAY

WINDSOR AVENUE

WINDSOR LANE

PRESTON ROAD

WINDSOR PARKWAY

SHANNON   LANE

CITY LIMIT

STANHOPE AVENUE

DALLAS COUNTRY CLUB

SHENANDOAH AVENUE

YMCA

NORMANDY AVENUE

CONNERLY AVENUE

DRIVE

N

SAN CARLOS DRIVE

ST.   ANDREWS

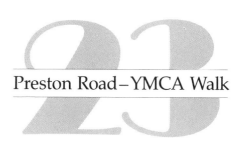

Preston Road–YMCA Walk

IT'S A GATHERING place for people of all ages in the Park Cities community—the Park Cities–North Dallas YMCA at 6000 Preston Road. From preschool classes to senior citizens' exercise and educational programs, the "Y" fills the fitness needs of many. Its facilities include the Seay Natatorium with a large indoor pool and small outdoor wading pool, a Nautilus Fitness Center, racquetball courts, a fully equipped gymnasium, and exercise and meeting rooms.

Programs such as Indian Guides and Indian Princesses are sponsored through the YMCA, as well as the youth sports program, which includes soccer, basketball, football, T-ball, and baseball for kindergarteners through sixth grade. The "Y" also offers progressive swim classes, exercise and aerobics classes for all ages, and several swim teams. Other classes include gymnastics for all levels, karate for adults and children, prenatal exercise classes, dog obedience, and such self improvement courses as stress management, CPR, and smoking cessation.

For senior citizens, the "Y" offers a program called Prime Time 55+, which includes a pool membership, social activities, and fitness classes in addition to other special privileges. And the pool is available for birthday party rentals by "Y" members who call well in advance. Office hours for the YMCA are Monday-Thursday 8:30 A.M.–9:00 P.M.; Friday 8:30 A.M.–8:00 P.M.; and Saturday 8:30 A.M.–5:00 P.M. The telephone number is 526-7293. No Park Cities walking book would be complete without mention of the YMCA, an active part of the community it serves.

Preston Road-YMCA Walk

THE MYTHICAL Ixion was tied to an endlessly revolving wheel, just as we often feel we are with our carpools, commuting to work, errands, appointments, and so on. Confined behind the wheel we lose sight of the beauty around us, the smell of the earth after a rain, the feel of the grass under our feet. Have you ever tried to see a sculpture at thirty miles an hour? Or watch a bird, or observe carefully the style of a house at that speed? It's the walkers, not the Ixions, who see the subtleties of nature, the beauty of a single flower, the forgotten cornerstone that commemorates the hope and toil of our ancestors. Take this walk for the sheer joy of it. It's a walk that begins on a trail that dates back to pre-Columbian times when, if you wanted to go anywhere, your feet had to take you.

Start your walk at the corner of Preston and Normandy, in front of the Park Cities-North Dallas YMCA. Here you'll see the first Texas historical marker in the entire Park Cities, marking this trace that existed for hundreds of years as a route for American Indians who ventured to another world. It follows the watershed between the Elm Fork and the East Fork of the Trinity River and was chosen because there are no large streams to cross. This early route continued to be used in later years by the Caddo Indians and was part of a Shawnee trail. Hardy pioneers like John Neely Bryan came down this trail in 1842, and thousands of longhorn steers on their way to the Chisholm trail went up it.

The trail is now called Preston Road, the first paved road in the Park Cities, named for William G. Preston, a Republic of Texas army captain. In the 1840s the Republic of Texas staked out a military highway on this trail from their capital in Austin to Fort Preston on the Red River. It was supposed to be a class "A" road, which meant there were to be no stumps over twelve feet high in the "highway." Today's Ixions would have had some choice words about that road! Before you drive Highway 289 north to rediscover the trail to Fort Preston, be forewarned that when Denison Dam was finished, Fort Preston and the northern end of Preston Road disappeared under Lake Texoma.

To commemorate this historic trail, for many years a group of riders and wagons annually descended Preston Road, arriving the Friday before the State Fair opened. All the Hyer School children would watch as this colorful group would pause for their final rest stop at Smith Park, across from Hyer School and the University Park United Methodist Church. These riders no longer come, but Preston Road has been permanently commemorated with the official Texas historical marker placed there in 1968.

The Park Cities YMCA hasn't always been located here. Its first building was the remodeled home of Judge J. N. Townsend at 3802 University, located at Goar Park close to the University Park City Hall, near where the gazebo stands today. Before that time the "Y" offered programs to the youth from a car, a sports version of the old book-mobile. There were 160 charter sports enthusiasts who supported this early program.

The First Unitarian Church owned the property the YMCA founders wanted to build on, where the "Y" stands today. Civic leader Karl Hoblitzelle owned the land east of Preston between Normandy and St. Andrews, so he struck a deal with the church. In exchange for some of his own property on Normandy plus some cash, he obtained the land between Normandy and Shenandoah. A few years later, in 1949, the church built the first of several buildings on Preston. You can see the cornerstone on the Normandy side of their building.

Hoblitzelle then donated the land for the "Y," and money was raised in a campaign in 1947 for a building. This building in front of you opened in 1951, with a cornerstone in memory of Hoblitzelle's wife, Esther, near the front steps. On the front of the building you'll see some bronze plaques bearing the names of many of the citizens who have had a part in making the "Y" such an integral part of the lives of Park Cities families today. In order to keep up with the growing needs of its sports- and health-minded families, these facilities have been remodeled and expanded several times, through the generosity of community leader Charles Seay and other benefactors. The youth sports program is

These young sports enthusiasts are shown standing in front of the first YMCA building in Goar Park in 1946. In 1951 the "Y"

dedicated to building character as well as fostering sports skills.

Turn on Normandy Avenue, just south of the YMCA, and walk east, veering to the right at Connerly to stay on Normandy. This route will take you from the busy hum of the voracious gas guzzlers to a surprisingly serene area just a few steps away. Perhaps the significance of this residential area is not in the architectural importance of a particular home or the exclusiveness of a country club, but as an example of the islands of serenity that can be found not far from your own doorstep if you take the time to look for them. This is an ideal walk for all ages—for a summer's bike outing with the children, or an early morning stroll before the day's chores impinge upon you.

Turn right on St. Andrews, where you'll see a Spanish home at 5929. This stucco house was built in 1924 by David Williams and shows the Spanish influence evident in his

moved to its expanded home at 6000 Preston Road. *Courtesy of the First RepublicBank Park Cities*

Karl Hoblitzelle, who donated the land on Preston Road to the YMCA, is shown presenting the deed to the site of the proposed new Park Cities YMCA building that opened in 1951. *Courtesy of the Park Cities–North Dallas YMCA*

early houses in its arches, carved stone columns on the second-story windows, and red tile roof. (For more on David Williams, see the Loma Linda Walk.)

Continue to 4004 St. Andrews, just around the bend, to see theater magnate and philanthropist Karl Hoblitzelle's former home, built in 1925. The estate encircling the Hoblitzelles' big white Colonial Revival home extended from St. Andrews to Normandy to Preston before he gave most of it away. Hoblitzelle donated the red brick building toward the west at 4012 St. Andrews to the First Unitarian Church, which uses it as a parish house, and sold the church the land between it and Preston at well below market cost. A tall, handsome man, Hoblitzelle was often seen in his later years striding down the street walking his two big dogs, a striking figure with white hair and white felt cowboy hat, surveying the community he loved.

Return east on St. Andrews across Normandy, and follow St. Andrews as it curves around to Westwick. Keeping Dallas Country Club on your right, turn right on Westwick, right again on Shannon Lane, and follow Shannon as it winds toward McFarlin. Hoblitzelle might have taken this very path while walking his dogs. As you meander along these streets enjoying the beautiful homes and the great care with which they are landscaped with seasonal color, you'll see evidence of the creeks that provided water to thirsty travelers or served as hiding places from Indians. Along these banks some boys once found buffalo bones that were hundreds of years old. Take this time to immerse yourself in the sights and sounds that the Ixions miss.

As you near McFarlin Boulevard the Gothic spire of the Highland Park Presbyterian Church will begin to come into view. The church's influence in the community is as far-reaching as its structure is imposing. Its congregation is the largest of any Presbyterian church in the United States, and one of the largest in the world. A walk around the huge facility will give you an idea of the extent of its programs.

Veer to your left at McFarlin to follow Shannon Lane around the west end of the church to University Boulevard. Oilman and philanthropist Herbert Hunt gave $3 million toward the new wing in memory of his mother, Lyda Bunker Hunt, for whom the building is named. She was deeply religious and a tremendous force in that family. Known as a dedicated member of this church and a hard

This photo taken in 1941 facing south on Hunters Glen near the intersection of Turtle Creek Boulevard shows the Highland Park Presbyterian Church sanctuary under construction. *Courtesy of Mr. and Mrs. George T. Lee, Jr.*

worker, she was frequently seen in the church kitchen lending a hand. Often Mrs. Hunt had Circle meetings at her home. As a child Herbert raised chickens and one day he walked into a Circle meeting to sell fresh eggs to the amused ladies in attendance.

Turn right on University and walk east, noting the name on the front of the west wing. Then continue east past the main sanctuary, built in 1941, with its magnificent arched stained glass window. To the east of the sanctuary some continuous arches are filled with stained glass. These are part of the first church building, which was named for the first full-time minister, Dr. W. A. Alexander. The 190 charter members met in what was then Highland Park High School (now McCulloch Middle School) until the Alexander Building was completed in 1928 at a cost of $75,000. The main sanctuary was built in 1941 during the ministry of Dr. H. W. DuBose, a popular money-raiser. After the sanctuary was constructed, arches were built to tie the buildings together. The architect for the entire Gothic church with its steep roofs, pointed arches, and stained glass windows was Mark Lemmon, who had designed another fine example of Gothic-style architecture as well, the Highland Park United Methodist Church.

In 1944 Dr. William Elliott, Jr., began his inspired ministry and the congregation tripled in membership before his retirement in 1973. The addition to the north and east of the Alexander Building in 1966 was called the Elliott Building.

Turn right on Park Street and continue around the church to see the two buildings on the McFarlin side that were added in the fifties. If it's hard to distinguish between buildings it's because they have been so artfully connected.

At the southeast corner of the church, stop and look to your left across McFarlin to view another David Williams home at 3805 McFarlin, next to the creek. It was the last private residence David Williams built and is characteristic of his more mature style. In 1983 this home was named by the Texas Society of Architects as one of the twenty most important architectural achievements in the state. (For more on this house, see the Turtle Creek Walk.) Williams was particularly concerned about the architectural integrity of his homes. When a new owner added a metal awning over a west window, Williams stopped by to introduce himself and tell them he wanted that metal awning removed! Eventually the owners did remove it.

Walk west on McFarlin to Shannon Lane. A left turn on Shannon and again on Windsor Parkway, where it says "Dead End," will lead you to a unique O'Neil Ford home blended into its environment at 3831 Windsor Parkway. Trees not only surround the house and grow out of the driveway, but also rise out of an interior courtyard. O'Neil Ford worked with David Williams for many years in the Dallas area developing the indigenous Texas architecture for which they became famous. Ford always felt more comfortable in the laid-back environment of San Antonio, where he designed Trinity University, although occasionally he would accept a commission in Dallas after he had moved his practice to San Antonio. Rather than period-style homes, Ford and Williams both preferred rambling homes of local materials with a practical concern for siting and Texas weather.

Choose your own route to return to the YMCA and Preston Road. Enjoy this verdant Texas environment, as your feet carry you forward to discover sights and sounds you've been too busy to notice, before the Ixion in you surfaces and takes over.

Time Line

A Capsule History

1836   Republic of Texas founded
1842   John Neely Bryan builds log cabin
1843   John Cole, Highland Park's first physician, arrives
1845   Texas annexed to the United States
1848   William Caruth arrives in Dallas
1849   Frances Sims Daniel arrives from Alabama
1850   Daniel Cemetery founded;
        First U.S. census
1852   Caruth moves to farm near Northwest Highway and Airline
1855   City of Dallas incorporated
1865   Highland Park's famous pecan tree planted
1870   Caruth Hill construction begun
1872   Railroad arrives in Dallas
1890   Exall Lake dammed
1897   Dallas Golf and Country Club formed
1899   First car in Dallas
1906   John Armstrong purchases land for Highland Park
1907   Highland Park opens
1911   Dallas chosen as location for SMU
1912   Dallas Hall construction begun;
        Highland Park Pharmacy founded;
        Dallas Country Club moves to Highland Park
1913   Highland Park incorporated
1914   Armstrong School opens;
        Highland Park Independent School District established
1915   SMU opens

1922   First high school built (now McCulloch
           Middle School);
           Katy Railroad Station opens on Knox
1924   University Park incorporated;
           Highland Park West opens;
           Loma Linda walls built;
           Highland Park Town Hall formally opened
1926   Bradfield School opens
1927   Snider Plaza opens
1928   University Park School opens
1930   Highland Park Library opens
1931   Highland Park Village opens
1936   Highland Park High School opens
1949   Hyer School opens
1951   Armstrong School burns;
           YMCA opens on Preston Road
1968   Katy Railroad Station closes
1986   Costello house moved to Old City Park

Did You Know?

DID YOU KNOW that the original city planners of Highland Park opposed building any churches in their elite community? They felt that the imposing structure of a church would be detrimental to the exclusiveness and elegance of the neighborhood and would depreciate the value of the residential area. Instead, they encouraged the churches to be built on the outskirts of the town. All the churches in the Park Cities are located in University Park, even though many of them bear the name Highland Park. (Part of the Highland Park United Methodist Church is in Highland Park.)

Did you know that University Park is the largest city in the state of Texas, and one of the largest in the U.S., without its own library?

Did you know that the motto of Armstrong School's Class of 1931 was "Be sure you are right, then go ahead"?

Did you know that in the twenties Dallas called Highland Park's football players the "silk stocking boys"? The games between Dallas and Highland Park caused so many riots between the spectators that Dallas banned all games with that opponent.

Did you know that Texas has more species of birds to see than any other state in the U.S., with California coming in a distant second? Three-fourths of all the birds found in the U.S. can be seen here, more than 540 species.

Did you know that in 1924 University Park's police department consisted of one policeman, Sam Hyman, who rode a motorcycle? The fire department had one fire truck driven by some of SMU's football players who lived at the fire station.

Did you know that every tree in the Park Cities has been planted, except for a few indigenous trees that were growing along Turtle and Hackberry Creeks?

Did you know that one fully grown tree can filter twenty thousand tons of pollution from the air within a growing season? But Highland Park alone is losing five hundred trees per year. An extensive survey of the "forestry" of the area indicated that there were too many crape myrtles and hackberries. Highland Park Judge Pat Robertson started a "Trees for the Town" project for the Park Cities to replace the trees that were dying with needed varieties. For a small fee you can purchase a tree that the city will plant, including red oaks, sweet gums, bur oaks, pecans, cedar elms, and Chinese pistachios. Call 522-2788 for more information.

Did you know that Highland Park is "wet" and University Park is "dry"?

Did you know that the *Park Cities News* was founded in January, 1938? Early Park Cities residents could hardly wait to read their small-town weekly from cover to cover, starting with the Police Reports. Sometimes free, sometimes under a different title, the *News* has developed into a prize-winning paper under its current owner, Marjorie Waters. January, 1988, marked its fiftieth anniversary.

Did you know that another local newspaper, *Park Cities People*, was founded in 1981 on the theory that the Park Cities didn't want a newspaper, they wanted a fan magazine starring themselves?

Did you know that there is a lighted flagpole in the Park Cities that flies the U.S. flag twenty-four hours a day, located west of Highlander Stadium?

Did you know that a newspaper columnist in Houston once said of Highland Park, "There is Highland Park and heaven, although occasionally the locals get the two mixed up"?

Sources

Acheson, Sam. *Dallas Yesterday*. Dallas: SMU Press, 1977.

American Institute of Architects. *Dallasights*. Dallas, 1978.

Brooks, Evelyn A. *Dallas: Yesterday and Today, A Social Studies Workbook for Third Grade*. Dallas: Banks Upshaw and Company, 1958.

Brooks, H. Allen. *Frank Lloyd Wright and the Prairie School*. New York: George Braziller, Inc., 1984.

Caruth, Mrs. W. W. Letter to her family found in her safety deposit box upon her death, December 12, 1958.

City of University Park Citizen Handbook. Dallas: City of University Park, 1985.

Dallas Newspaper Artists' Association. *Makers of Dallas*. Dallas, 1912.

Dealey, Ted. *Diaper Days of Dallas*. Nashville: Avingdon Press, 1966.

Dillon, David. *Dallas Architecture, 1936–1986*. Austin: Texas Monthly Press, 1985.

Goodman, Lorraine. *Greenway Parks—A Special Place*. Dallas: Lorraine Goodman, 1980.

Greene, A. C. *Dallas, The Deciding Years*. Austin: Encino Press, 1973.

History of the Highland Park Presbyterian Church, 1926–1967. Dallas: 1967.

Johnson, Doris Miller. *Golden Prologue to the Future, A History of the Highland Park Methodist Church*. Nashville: Parthenon Press, 1966.

Lankford, La Vern. *Historical Notes on the Park Cities*. Dallas: 1979.

McAlester, Virginia and Lee. *A Field Guide to American Houses*. New York: Alfred A. Knopf, 1986.

McCarthy, Muriel. *David R. Williams: Pioneer Architect*. Dallas: SMU Press, 1983.

McDonald, W. L. *Dallas Rediscovered*. Dallas: Dallas Historical Society, 1978.

Moore, Doris Dowdell. *Signs of His Presence*. Dallas: Highland Park United Methodist Church, 1975.

Payne, Darwin. *Dallas: An Illustrated History*. Woodland Hills, California: Windsor Publications, 1982.

Rogers, J. W. *Lusty Texans of Dallas*. New York: E. P. Dutton and Company, Inc., 1951.

"Seventy-Five Years Later: The State of the Dream," *Southern Methodist University 1986 Annual Report*. Dallas: Southern Methodist University, 1986.

SMU Mustang Magazine, ed. Patricia Ann LaSalle. Dallas: SMU Alumni Association, Fall 1986.

Stephens, Phil. "Park Cities Heritage, Past, Present and Future," *Park Cities People*. Dallas: Vol. 7, No. 3, January 15, 1987.

Stimson, Vernelle. *The History of the John S. Armstrong School, 1914–1974*. Dallas, 1974.

The First Fifty Years. Dallas: Highland Park Presbyterian Church, 1976.

The Story of the City of University Park. Dallas: City of University Park, 1967.

Trezevant, J. T. "History of Dallas Country Club." Dallas, 1913.

White, James F. *Architecture at SMU*. Dallas: SMU Press, 1966.

Wineburgh, H. Harold. *The Texas Banker: The Life and Times of Fred F. Florence*. Dallas, 1981.

Index

247